Business Communication

Fourth Edition

A. C. "Buddy" Krizan
Murray State University

Patricia Merrier
University of Minnesota, Duluth

Carol Larson Jones
California State Polytechnic University, Pomona

Jules Harcourt
Murray State University

 South-Western College Publishing
an International Thomson Publishing company ITP®

Cincinnati · Albany · Boston · Detroit · Johannesburg · London · Madrid · Melbourne · Mexico City
New York · Pacific Grove · San Francisco · Scottsdale · Singapore · Tokyo · Toronto

Publishing Team Director: Dave Shaut

Developmental/Aquisitions Editor: Amy Villanueva

Production Editor: Kelly Keeler

Manufacturing Coordinator: Sue Kirven

Marketing Manager: Sarah Woelfel

Copyright © 1999
by SOUTH-WESTERN COLLEGE PUBLISHING
Cincinnati, Ohio

All Rights Reserved
The text of this publication, or any part thereof, may not be reproduced in any manner
whatsoever for any other purpose without prior written permission of the publisher.

4 5 PN 2 1 0
Printed in the United States of America

ISBN: 0-538- 88823-7

I(T)P®
International Thomson Publishing
South-Western College Publishing is an ITP Company. The ITP trademark is used under license.

CONTENTS

PART 1   THE COMMUNICATION ENVIRONMENT

Chapter 1   Business Communication Foundations. 1

Chapter 2   International and Cross-Cultural Business Communication 7

Chapter 3   Communication Technologies and Techniques 11

PART 2   DEVELOPING COMMUNICATIONS

Chapter 4   Principles of Business Communication 15

Chapter 5   Developing Effective and Ethical Business Messages. 23

PART 3   CORRESPONDENCE APPLICATIONS

Chapter 6   Positive and Neutral Messages. 29

Chapter 7   Goodwill Messages 35

Chapter 8   Negative Messages. 41

Chapter 9   Persuasive Messages 49

PART 4   EMPLOYMENT COMMUNICATION

Chapter 10   The Job Search and Resume 55

Chapter 11   Employment Communication and Interviewing 61

PART 5   WRITTEN REPORT APPLICATIONS

Chapter 12   Research Techniques and Proposals 67

Chapter 13   Report Preparation 75

Chapter 14   Graphic Aids 81

PART 6   ORAL AND NONVERBAL COMMUNICATION

Chapter 15   Listening and Nonverbal Messages 87

Chapter 16   Oral Communication Essentials 91

Chapter 17   Oral Communication Applications 97

CHAPTER 1

Business Communication Foundations

LEARNING ACTIVITIES

True or False?

Circle T if the statement is true; circle F if the statement is false.

T   F   **1.** The ability to communicate effectively will influence your career success.

T   F   **2.** Both internal and external communication are important to business success.

T   F   **3.** The most important goal in business communication is receiver response.

T   F   **4.** The sender has primary responsibility for achieving the four goals of business communication.

T   F   **5.** The basic patterns of business communication are downward, horizontal, upward, and serial.

T   F   **6.** Informal communication can be work-related or personal.

T   F   **7.** Network communication can extend into individuals' personal lives.

T   F   **8.** Using face-to-face oral communication will assure accuracy in serial communication.

T   F   **9.** Detailed job instructions can best be communicated by using an oral message.

T   F   **10.** The sender has a responsibility to help receivers overcome any physical or mental disabilities they may have that cause communication barriers.

Multiple Choice

In the blank at the left, write the letter that represents the best response.

_____ **1.** Business communication can be defined as
   a. all contacts inside and outside an organization.
   b. establishing a common understanding within a business environment.
   c. preparing letters and memos.
   d. the transmission of data and information in the business environment.

_____ **2.** The most important business communication goal is that the
   a. receiver provides the necessary response to the sender.
   b. receiver understands the message as the sender intended.
   c. sender and the receiver maintain a favorable relationship.
   d. sender's organization gains goodwill.

_____ **3.** In networking, communication flows
   a. diagonally.
   b. downward.
   c. horizontally.
   d. upward.

_____ **4.** The most effective words for a sender to use in a business message are
   a. technical words.
   b. words below the receiver's reading level.
   c. words in the receiver's vocabulary.
   d. words that challenge the receiver.

_____ **5.** Formal communication in an organization
   a. flows in all directions
   b. is essential for effective personal relationships.
   c. is not essential for the operation of a business.
   d. is not planned by the organization.

_____ **6.** While the use of proper grammar in messages is important, it will NOT
   a. aid receiver understanding.
   b. assure sender success.
   c. help maintain sender credibility.
   d. improve receiver acceptance.

_____ **7.** An inference is
   a. a conclusion drawn by a receiver.
   b. a form of feedback.
   c. a suggestion made by a sender.
   d. a word meaning derived from a receiver's experience.

_____ **8.** The receiver
   a. has no responsibility in the communication process.
   b. has primary responsibility for the success of the communication process.
   c. selects the communication channel.
   d. should be open to different types of senders.

9. Oral messages should be used when
   a. immediate feedback is desired.
   b. it is desirable to have a record of the communication.
   c. the message is complex.
   d. transmission speed is not a concern.

10. Which of the following is NOT an appropriate method for obtaining feedback to an oral presentation?
   a. Asking the audience to complete an evaluation form
   b. Asking questions
   c. Doing a self-evaluation
   d. Observing the audience

Completion

Complete each item by writing the necessary word or words.

1. A receiver may respond to a message with _____, _____, or _____.

2. Three important ways for a sender to maintain a favorable relationship with a receiver are:

   a. _____

   b. _____

   c. _____

3. The sender and receiver should relate to each other _____, _____, and _____.

4. The major patterns of business communication are _____, _____, _____, and _____.

5. The communication environment includes the _____, the _____, the _____, and the _____.

6. The two basic types of communication are _____ and _____.

7. The receiver should be analyzed in four areas: _____, _____, _____, and _____.

8. The receiver's values, opinions, biases, prejudices, and viewpoints are examples of the receiver's _____—the third category to be analyzed by the sender.

9. The primary purpose of analyzing the receiver is to enable you to use the _____.

10. You–viewpoint messages respect and emphasize the receiver's _____ and _____.

11. Words can have both _____ and _____ meanings.

12. Communication barriers are any factors that _____

_____.

13. Inferences may be drawn from _____ and _____.

14. List four examples of communication barriers that should be removed so that effective communication can take place.

_____, _____,

_____, and _____.

15. The appearance of a message affects its _____ and influences a receiver's
_____ of its content.

Matching

Write the letter of the best answer in the blank preceding the description. Some answers may be used more than once; others may not be used at all.

_____ **1.** The most important business communication goal	**a.** communication channels
	b. favorable relationship
_____ **2.** Memos, e-mail, conversations	
	c. grapevine
_____ **3.** Results in the diagonal flow of information	**d.** honesty
_____ **4.** Message passed along between three or more people	**e.** network
	f. oral message
_____ **5.** Informal communication	
	g. planned communication
_____ **6.** Primarily responsible for communication success	**h.** receiver
_____ **7.** Provides greater opportunity for feedback	**i.** receiver benefits
	j. receiver response
_____ **8.** Central focus of you–viewpoint	**k.** receiver understanding
_____ **9.** Basic to successful communication	**l.** serial communication
_____ **10.** Formal communication	**m.** sender

Review Questions

1. Explain why business communication is important to individuals.

2. List the four goals of business communication and explain how to achieve each.

3. Indicate the roles of the sender and the receiver in the communication process.

4. Select a person known both to you and to your instructor and analyze that person as a receiver of messages.

5. Create five 1-sentence examples of the use of the I–viewpoint. Revise each sentence so that it reflects the you–viewpoint.

APPLICATION EXERCISES

Revise the following sentences so they reflect you–viewpoint writing.

1. We were pleased to receive your application for a business loan.

2. You failed to enclose your check with your letter to us.

3. I am sorry we cannot repair your car until Friday.

4. The First National Bank now has a 24-hour teller machine at the Rivercity Mall.

5. It is impossible to sell you a new car before your credit is approved.

6. We proudly manufacture high-quality merchandise.

7. Closing your account with us is a mistake because Jefferson's is going to lower its prices soon.

8. You should move quickly or you will miss the sale of the year.

9. We are glad that you purchase all of your gasoline at Benson's.

10. You should be aware that Kenwell's does not make refunds on food items that have been removed from their original package.

11. We want to be sure that our service is the best, and you can help us by stopping by our store and completing our questionnaire.

12. I am pleased to approve your request for a salary increase.

13. It is too bad about the terrible problems you are experiencing.

14. Selling toll-free 24 hours per day is our business. You can call us any time at 1 (800) 555–1122.

15. Please write me, and let me know what color to send.

CHAPTER 2

International and Cross-Cultural Business Communication

LEARNING ACTIVITIES

True or False?

Circle T if the statement is true; circle F if the statement is false.

T   F   **1.** Most students today will be involved in international and cross-cultural business communication at some time during their careers.

T   F   **2.** *Americans* is a term used throughout the world to refer to citizens of the United States.

T   F   **3.** More than 20,000 languages are spoken throughout the world.

T   F   **4.** American manufacturers have made serious, costly errors because of their lack of knowledge of other cultures.

T   F   **5.** There is less variation in nonverbal signals than there is in language.

T   F   **6.** Some acceptable and common nonverbal signals in one culture may be vulgar in another culture.

T   F   **7.** The way that people feel and think is the most important cultural difference in cross-cultural communication.

T   F   **8.** The goal of cross-cultural communication is to achieve normal business communication without cultural prejudice.

T   F   **9.** The key guideline for cross-cultural communication is to analyze your own culture.

T   F   **10.** Stereotypes of other cultures are largely inaccurate and not useful.

T   F   **11.** The study of cultural relativism indicates that there is not necessarily one right or wrong way to do something—merely many different, but equally correct, ways.

T   F   **12.** If you know only a few words of another person's language, it is better not to use them until you know enough of the language to construct sentences.

T   F   **13.** When using an interpreter, be careful of the words you use and ask the interpreter to convey the spirit of your message, not just the literal meaning.

T   F   **14.** "When in Rome do as the Romans do," is an appropriate adage for international businesspersons to follow.

T   F   **15.** High-quality translation software is available to translate from one language to another.

Multiple Choice

In the blank at the left, write the letter that represents the best answer.

_____ **1.** The number of cultures estimated to exist in the world is
    a. 2,000.
    b. 5,000.
    c. 10,000.
    d. 20,000.

_____ **2.** In Japan the most acceptable nonverbal greeting is
    a. shaking hands.
    b. an embrace.
    c. a bow.
    d. the wai.

_____ **3.** Among the following cultural attributes, the one(s) the Japanese value most highly is/are
    a. individual achievement.
    b. human relationships.
    c. directness.
    d. business relationships.

_____ **4.** Most international business communication is conducted in
    a. Spanish.
    b. English.
    c. French.
    d. German.

_____ **5.** The culture that is least likely to base moral judgments on absolute ethical standards is
    a. American.
    b. Canadian.
    c. German.
    d. Japanese.

_____ **6.** The culture that is most likely to have members who are basically conservative and who prefer discipline and order to change is
    a. American.
    b. Canadian.
    c. German.
    d. Japanese.

_____ 7. The United States' largest trading partner is
  a. Canada.
  b. Mexico.
  c. Japan.
  d. Germany.

_____ 8. Mexicans are likely to achieve self-esteem primarily through
  a. approval of superiors.
  b. friendships and personal relationships.
  c. achievement on the job.
  d. individual accomplishment.

_____ 9. The core dimension(s) of diversity that may be considered relatively immutable or inborn is (are)
  a. age and gender.
  b. ethnicity and race.
  c. physical abilities.
  d. all of the above.

_____ 10. The source of information that most likely publishes most extensively on cross-cultural communication is
  a. Association for Business Communication.
  b. International Association of Business Communicators.
  c. David M. Kennedy Center for International Studies.
  d. International Business Publishing Company.

Matching

Write the letter of the best answer in the blank preceding the term. Each answer may be used only once.

_____ 1. Bow

_____ 2. "Marks" in Canada

_____ 3. Wai

_____ 4. Namaste

_____ 5. Australian emu

_____ 6. Chinese

_____ 7. Eye contact

_____ 8. American Indians

_____ 9. Personal trust

_____ 10. Organizational performance

  a. bird

  b. stoic

  c. bending gently with palms together below chin

  d. bending at the waist

  e. greeting in Thailand

  f. valuing diversity

  g. more important in Japan than business relations

  h. necessary in France

  i. Cultural Revolution

  j. school grades

  k. upward movement of the head

Completion

Complete each item by writing the necessary word or words.

1. Cross-cultural communication means communication between members of _____.

2. *Cultural relativism* means that different cultures have different _____.

3. The variation among receivers' cultures in the world includes differences in _____, _____, and _____. (List only three.)

4. Members of the Japanese culture practice _____ ethics.

5. When communicating with Germans, Americans should generally be _____, _____, _____, and _____.

6. In international business communication, there is as much variation among the meanings of _____ signals as there is variation among languages.

7. The most important difference among cultures to consider in cross-cultural communication is the way people _____.

8. In cross-cultural communication situations, the basic business communication knowledge you have already gained (will, will not) _____ apply.

9. A starting point in preparing yourself to communicate with persons from another culture is Guideline 2: _____.

10. Eye contact while conversing is a sign of _____ and _____ to Americans.

Review Questions

1. Why are American businesses becoming more involved in world trade?

2. Describe the language differences throughout the world.

3. Describe the differences in nonverbal signals throughout the world.

4. List the five dimensions of human diversity and explain the importance of understanding these dimensions.

5. Describe the differences in business hours and days in countries throughout the world.

6. To be successful in international and cross-cultural business communication, you are encouraged to learn all you can about other cultures and then apply what you learn. What are examples of the kinds of things you should learn about other cultures?

7. Give five examples of behavior appropriate for a business meeting with Japanese businesspersons.

8. Give five examples of behavior appropriate for a business meeting with German businesspersons.

9. How are citizens of Mexico different from citizens of the United States? Give five examples.

10. Explain how a Chinese name is written.

CHAPTER 3

Communication Technologies and Techniques

LEARNING ACTIVITIES

True or False?

Circle T if the statement is true; circle F if the statement is false.

T F **1.** Communicators rely on technology to help them create and convey messages.

T F **2.** Writers should incorporate as many enhancement features into a document as possible.

T F **3.** E-mail may be used to send a message locally or internationally.

T F **4.** Fax transmissions can be made using paper or a computer.

T F **5.** Data entered into a spreadsheet can often be converted into a visual aid.

T F **6.** Style checkers detect and correct grammar and punctuation errors.

T F **7.** E-mail is appropriate for both positive and negative messages.

T F **8.** Some emphasis techniques have special meaning in e-mail.

T F **9.** Interactive collaborative writing allows users to work on a document at their convenience.

T F **10.** Voice mail is a subset of groupware.

Completion

Complete each item by writing the necessary word or words.

1. A spell checker assists with but does not replace _____.

2. Writers who use word processing software should focus on _____ before _____.

3. The _____ feature of word processing software allow writers to insert _____ from a mailing list or directory into a message.

4. The _____ and spell checker are two popular features of word processing software.

5. An _____ message resembles a memo.

6. A video conference uses both _____ and _____.

7. Business e-mail messages should be edited based on the writer's analysis of the _____ and the _____.

8. Internet users _____ a listserv but _____ bulletin boards and chatrooms.

9. USENET is a service that allows Internet users to _____, _____, and _____.

10. _____ combine several software programs into one larger product.

Matching

Write the letter of the best answer in the blank preceding the term. Some answers may be used more than once; others may not be used at all.

_____ 1. Most common Internet application

_____ 2. Spreadsheet data location

_____ 3. Wireless message system

_____ 4. Converts printed text into electronic form

_____ 5. Listservs, bulletin boards, and chatrooms

_____ 6. Gives access to an e-mail address book listing

_____ 7. World's largest network

_____ 8. Creates tables and charts

_____ 9. Audio version of e-mail

_____ 10. Uses sound and animation

a. alias

b. audio conference

c. cell

d. cellular phone

e. e-mail

f. graphics software

g. groupware

h. Intranet

i. Internet

j. newsgroups

k. pager

l. scanner

m. telecommuter

n. voice mail

o. video conference

APPLICATION EXERCISE

After reading the following paragraphs, underline the errors that would not have been detected by a spell checker.

Tank your four at tending the in vestment seminar held on September 33. Mr. Amy Bockworth is an excellent presenter; you are confident you grained much from her presentation.

Ms. Bockworth indicated hat you were interested in baying a copy of *Money Madness*, the book she rote. An order firm is enclosed. Simple return the farm with you check fore $12.9, and well process your order.

CHAPTER 4

Principles of Business Communication

LEARNING ACTIVITIES

True or False?

Circle T if the statement is true; circle F if the statement is false.

T   F   **1.** The basic principle of business communication is the KISS principle.

T   F   **2.** A thesaurus is a way of finding the simplest and most precise words for a message.

T   F   **3.** For senders and receivers in the same occupation, technical words cannot assist in conveying more effective messages.

T   F   **4.** In some situations negative words can be used for emphasis.

T   F   **5.** Abstract words can be useful if a sender wants to de-emphasize an idea.

T   F   **6.** In letters and memos, a sentence should be considered long if it is 15 words or more.

T   F   **7.** One way to limit content in sentences is to add commas and semicolons to long sentences to make them more readable.

T   F   **8.** A sentence formed in such a way that the subject is acted upon is said to be written in active voice.

T   F   **9.** "Men are 27 percent stronger than women," is an example of biased language.

T   F   **10.** The English language has a gender-biased structure.

Completion

Complete each item by writing the necessary word or words.

1. The best way to improve your ability to compose effective business messages is to learn and use the _____ of business communication.

2. The two most valuable resources or references for the business communicator are a _____ and a _____.

3. The most effective words you can choose for your messages are those words that your receiver will _____ and that will secure the _____.

4. Words that are understandable are words that are in your receiver's _____.

5. Words that have special meanings in a particular field are called _____.

6. Concrete words are _____; abstract words are _____.

7. The strongest words, or parts of speech, in the English language are _____ and _____.

8. A sentence that has _____ contains one main idea—one thought.

9. Use of the generic word *man* _____.

10. Any sentence that exceeds _____ words should be considered a long sentence and should be examined for clarity.

11. In developing sentences, the principle "keep related words together" means that modifiers should be placed _____.

12. Biased language offends _____ and _____.

13. If any paragraph in a letter or memo is _____ lines or more, it is considered long.

14. In business report writing, paragraphs can average _____ lines.

15. _____ lines or more in any paragraph in a report is long.

Review Questions

1. What are concrete words? Why should you use them in your business communication?

2. What is the difference between strong and weak words? Which are preferred in business communication?

3. Explain the impact of the use of negative words in business messages.

4. Explain how to implement Principle 8: Use Short Sentences. Include in your explanation the recommendation regarding sentence length—short, average, and long—for letters and memos and for reports.

5. What is the difference between the active voice and passive voice in sentences? When should the active voice be used and when should the passive voice be used?

6. Explain what Principle 6: Avoid Obsolete Words means.

7. Explain the direct plan and the indirect plan for organizing paragraphs.

8. Explain how you can use transitional words to provide paragraph coherence.

9. What are the three basic types of tie-in sentences that can be used to provide paragraph coherence?

10. Explain how the use of a dictionary can help you be a more effective communicator.

APPLICATION EXERCISES

Assume for these exercises that your receiver is a college freshman with a vocabulary at about the 11th- to 12th-grade level. Your receiver is majoring in business administration. Be sure to retain the basic meaning of the original words in your revisions. Use examples different from those used in the textbook. Use your dictionary and thesaurus to assist you in these exercises.

1. Select words that will be more *familiar* to your receiver.

   a. verbalize   _____

   b. utilize   _____

   c. perspiration   _____

   d. gesticulate   _____

   e. facetious   _____

2. Choose *shorter* words.

   a. facilitate   _____

   b. lackadaisical   _____

   c. aberration   _____

   d. inaugurate   _____

   e. judicious   _____

3. As appropriate, replace these technical words with *familiar* words.

   a. generate   _____

   b. de facto   _____

   c. generic   _____

   d. format   _____

   e. expectorate   _____

4. Select words that are more *concrete*.

    a. book   _____

    b. country   _____

    c. office equipment   _____

5. Select words that are more *abstract*.

    a. 3:00 P.M., Wednesday   _____

    b. 18 times out of 20   _____

    c. would give your life for   _____

6. Choose *stronger* words.

    a. male parent   _____

    b. dismissed   _____

    c. requested   _____

7. Choose *weaker* words.

    a. demand   _____

    b. tactless   _____

    c. repossessed   _____

8. List three positive words and three negative words.

    a. _____   **a.** _____

    b. _____   **b.** _____

    c. _____   **c.** _____

9. Revise these sentences so they are more understandable.

    a. Her proficiency as a writer was incomparable.

    _____

    _____

    b. Fabricating data is fraudulent.

    _____

    _____

    c. Optimum arrangements were facilitated for financing Ping-ying's matriculation.

    _____

    _____

10. Revise these sentences so they are more positive.

    a. Our policy forbids refunds without the sales slip.

    _____

    _____

    b. We regret that you have decided to quit.

    _____

    _____

    c. Stop coming in late.

    _____

    _____

11. Rearrange these sentences so that the modifiers will be in more appropriate locations and the relationships will be clearer.

    a. If the fringe benefits are to be changed, employees before any action is taken will want to be consulted.

    _____

    _____

    b. Being in dilapidated condition, the ABC Wrecking Company demolished the factory building.

    _____

    _____

    c. All the employees were reprimanded who were late.

    _____

    _____

12. Shorten these sentences.

    a. While all the very fine communication equipment is helpful, it remains still very important to compose messages with conciseness and clarity and with clear sentences.

    _____

    _____

    b. The first and initial version of the word processing software was welcomed with open arms.

    _____

    _____

    c. This correspondence is the letter mailed to me, which I received through the mail yesterday.

    _____

    _____

13. Change the voice in these sentences from passive to active.

    a. A truck will be driven to Pleasanton by Sally Frahm.

    _____

    _____

    b. Finally, the memo was received in the chairperson's office.

    _____

    _____

    c. Lian Lian's concerns were listened to by the department chair.

    _____

    _____

14. Create sentences that give the emphasis specified.

    a. Emphasize the low cost of a personal stereo by the length of your sentence.

    _____

    _____

    b. Use format to emphasize the four goals of business communication you learned in Chapter 1.

    _____

    _____

    c. Use sentence structure to emphasize the date of a birthday and to de-emphasize the person's age.

    _____

    _____

15. Improve the unity of the following paragraph by identifying the sentence that does not belong.

When preparing for a job interview, you should learn all you can about the company, In addition, you should try to anticipate all possible questions. Be sure to be on time for the interview. Give attention to the clothes you will wear and your grooming. Possibly the most important preparation you will make is a mental one; a confident attitude is essential for success.

Sentence that does not belong: _____

_____

_____

_____

_____

16. Select the most logical order for these sentences so they will form a paragraph that uses the indirect plan.

    a. Join PBL today!

    b. These new skills and spirit will serve you well all your life.

c. What are the benefits of PBL membership?

d. Through membership you can strengthen your leadership skills and sharpen your competitive edge.

Order: (1) _____ (2) _____ (3) _____ (4) _____

17. Select the most logical order for the sentences in Exercise 16 using the direct plan.

Order: (1) _____ (2) _____ (3) _____ (4) _____

18. Provide coherence for the following paragraph by inserting the appropriate transitional words or tie-in sentences.

The personnel officer called and said she wanted to talk to Pete. She said he is being considered for a job. She said that the call was about an interview. She asked that Pete return the call. Her instructions were that he should do so as soon as possible.

With coherence:_____

_____

_____

_____

_____

_____

_____

_____

19. Restore coherence to the following paragraph by reordering the sentences so that they provide for a flow of thought and the logical movement of the reader's mind from one idea to the next. Indicate your order by placing the letters of the sentences in the blanks provided.

(a) To increase market share and gain the profit that goes with it, a business must have managers who are ethical, alert, tough, dynamic, creative, persevering, and energetic. (b) In fact, the market share must increase if a business is to grow and prosper. (c) Ways must continually be found to regain any lost market share and the profit that goes with it. (d) That environment includes the appearance of new competitors with new and better ideas for attracting customers. (e) These kinds of managers make profits and make businesses successful. (f) A business must make a profit to be successful. (g) This essential profit is fought for in a challenging, competitive environment. (h) These new competitors take a share of the market.

Order: (1) _____ (2) _____ (3) _____ (4) _____ (5) _____ (6) _____ (7) _____ (8) _____

20. Rewrite the well-intended but poorly written memo that follows. Apply the principles of business communication you have studied in this chapter. Include in your memo only the information you think is important for the bank employees to know about the new marketing program.

It is with a great deal of delight that I announce that the American National Bank is initiating a new marketing effort called the "Bank Marketing Program" that should cause an expansion of our services to materialize in the near future over the next few months in our market area of American and the surrounding counties. To internalize this plan through each employee learning his or her role in its implementation, we will all attend a American State University special course in the bank's Community Services Room designed exclusively for our employees that explicates the promotional concept and strategy. This course will begin soon. Now I know that it goes without saying that many of you do not want "to go to school" again, but attending this seminar is the only way that you can be adequately informed and enabled to support our important new effort that is vital to the sustenance of our bottom line position. On another topic, summer is just around the corner and many of you will be taking accumulated vacation leave time; and we should not schedule those during June when the Bank Marketing Course will be conducted.

Banking Promotions, Inc., designed this new program especially for us. They have been extremely successful in over 50 other communities. As per the previously stated comments, our efforts to cooperate and support and participate in the new marketing effort can result in strengthening our competitive position which, in turn, will stabilize and enhance our relative financial position, assure continued employment opportunities for all employees, and improve the picture for the employee profit sharing program. Trusting that I can count on your best efforts, good luck with the new "Bank Marketing Program."

CHAPTER 5

Developing Effective
and Ethical
Business Messages

LEARNING ACTIVITIES

True or False?

Circle T if the statement is true; circle F if the statement is false.

T   F   **1.** Step 1 in Planning and Composing Business Messages includes analyzing the receiver for the you–viewpoint.

T   F   **2.** When using the you-viewpoint, give highest priority to what you think will be your receiver's perception of the message.

T   F   **3.** An advantage of oral messages is that they are more personal.

T   F   **4.** You should use the direct plan for persuasive messages.

T   F   **5.** When drafting a message, it is important to get it just right in order to avoid editing, revising, and proofreading later.

T   F   **6.** The middle-level receiver's vocabulary will fall between grade levels 8 and 10.

T   F   **7.** Being ethical in your business communication includes striving for the highest good attainable for all those involved in the communication.

T   F   **8.** Because business communicators cannot be expected to know all the laws that affect their communication, they should ask that routine messages be reviewed by an attorney.

T   F   **9.** The Golden Rule is "Do unto others as you would have them do unto you."

T   F   **10.** Being ethical in your communication is not essential to a successful personal life and business career.

Multiple Choice

In the blank at the left, write the letter that represents the best answer.

_____ 1. The primary and secondary purposes of a message are the
   a. direct and indirect plans.
   b. main idea and supporting ideas.
   c. you–viewpoint and vocabulary level.
   d. first and second content items.

_____ 2. An advantage of a written message is that it
   a. is quickly transmitted.
   b. is more personal.
   c. allows immediate feedback.
   d. accommodates lengthy and complex content.

_____ 3. The indirect approach should be used for most messages that contain
   a. positive and neutral information.
   b. neutral and persuasive information.
   c. negative and persuasive information.
   d. positive and persuasive information.

_____ 4. The size and composition of the collaborative group will depend on
   a. the nature of the report, proposal, or other message that must be developed.
   b. the writing ability of the group members.
   c. the loyalty of the employees.
   d. the deadline date of the report, proposal, or other message.

_____ 5. When used in ethical decision making, the social utility concept requires a communicator to
   a. determine the greatest good and the least harm for all affected.
   b. follow the guidance of the standards of society at large.
   c. follow the universal law that applies.
   d. assess the situation using the Golden Rule.

_____ 6. Readability formulas
   a. indicate the vocabulary level at which a message is written.
   b. measure the average length of sentences, the percentage of difficult words in a message, and the accuracy of the message.
   c. check the actual words used in a message.
   d. determine the manner in which words are combined into sentences in messages.

_____ 7. Express warranties of products and services are established by
   a. salesperson statements to the customer.
   b. statements of the customer during a transaction.
   c. customer requests in writing.
   d. businesses putting guarantees in writing.

8. Employment communication is most influenced by which of the following pieces of legislation?
   a. Civil Rights Act
   b. Plain English laws
   c. Labor-Management Relations Act
   d. The Privacy Act

_____ 9. Ethical communication
   a. is not important in government offices
   b. strives for the highest good for all involved and provides information that is truthful
   c. is essential for only the Fortune 500 companies
   d. is possible today because of the Web

_____ 10. The Four-Way Test of Things We Think, Say, or Do, stresses:
   a. evaluation of an individual's business aptitutude
   b. universal law concepts
   c. the promotion of becoming a member of Rotary International, a service club
   d. truth, fairness, goodwill, good interpersonal relationships, and benefits to all concerned.

Completion

Complete each item by writing the necessary word or words.

1. The process for planning and composing all types of written and oral business messages is the same. The three steps in the process are:

   a. to determine _____.

   b. to analyze the receiver for the _____.

   c. to compose _____.

2. When a team of writers develops a message, the process is called _____
   _____

3. The first step in developing messages has two tasks:

   a. Analyze the _____.

   b. Establish _____ and _____ purposes.

4. The receiver should be analyzed in four areas:

   _____, _____,
   _____, and _____.

5. Using the you–viewpoint means choosing words that are _____
   and _____ to your receiver.

6. To achieve the purpose(s) of a message that will be sent to multiple receivers, the message should be composed at the _____ level that can be understood by all members of the group.

7. The receiver's _____ of your message is your message.

8. The three main advantages of oral messages are that they _____ _____, _____, and _____.

9. The two organizational plans for messages are the _____ plan and the _____ plan.

10. The two parts involved in the task of outlining message content are _____ _____ and _____.

11. After the content of the message has been outlined, the next task is to _____ the message.

12. When editing and revising, keep the _____ and _____ purposes of the message in mind.

13. Careful proofreading involves:

    a. reading the message for _____.

    b. reading it again for correct _____, _____, and _____.

14. A readability formula indicates the _____ _____ at which a message is written.

15. Business messages written at the _____ to the _____ grade levels will communicate clearly to most receivers.

16. Most high school graduates' vocabulary levels will be at grade levels _____ to _____.

17. Being ethical is doing what is _____ to achieve what is _____.

18. The _____ concept requires that communicators be willing to require all others to behave as they are behaving.

19. If you are not sure about the legality of one of your messages, you should consult an _____ or other _____.

20. To enhance teamwork, organizations are beginning to use computer-based _____ _____ to enable a group of participants to work interactively in an electronic environment.

APPLICATION EXERCISES

Improve the following sentences by editing and revising them. Correct all errors.

1. The soldiers they are tired and weary.

2. Once the plan is completed and the plan is finalized the plan will be submitted to management.

3. Communication has a power that, for all intents and purposes, is not equaled by anything else.

4. Do you think that it is time for a meeting so we can get together and discuss relevant and appropriate plans for new products?

5. At some point in the future, Paul will be put in line to be named president of the company.

6. Tri too finde thee problems in this sentince.

7. Schedulse help or ganizes the work

8. She think thet the produuction qota wil bea meet

9. The questions askt bi the student's wer good wones

10. is the end of maple street were marked withe a detoor sign

WORD PUZZLE

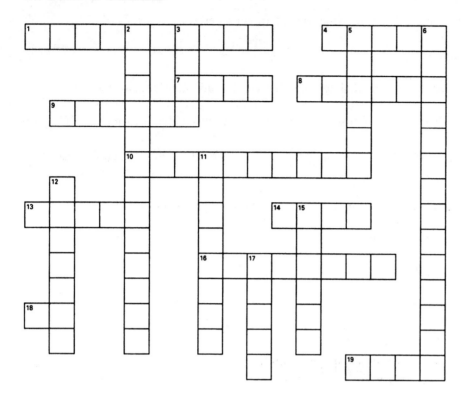

Across

1. The words that one knows

4. Lying that causes monetary damage

7. _____ processing equipment

8. Readability _____

9. Moral code or values

10. To put people in categories

13. Ethical philosophy

14. A way to strengthen a message

16. An organizational plan for a message

18. Male pronoun

19. The message's _____ idea is its primary purpose.

Down

2. Technique for creating ideas

3. Legal requirements

5. Edit and _____ messages

6. Prohibited by the Civil Rights Act

11. Listener or reader

12. Type of message

15. An organizational plan for a message

17. First effort at composing a message

CHAPTER 6

Positive and Neutral Messages

LEARNING ACTIVITIES

True or False?

Circle T if the statement is true; circle F if the statement is false.

T   F   **1.** Only positive words should be used in describing the positive news.

T   F   **2.** Even though a claim letter may contain negative information, the writer should present the message positively.

T   F   **3.** Persuasion may be needed in some inquiries about products.

T   F   **4.** One important advantage of using the direct plan for positive or neutral messages is that it gets the receiver in the proper frame of mind.

T   F   **5.** The you–viewpoint need not be considered in the sales appeal of a direct plan.

T   F   **6.** Questions in inquiries should be general in order to allow the respondent flexibility in answering.

T   F   **7.** In an adjustment message, the best place for an apology is in the close to help the receiver remember it.

T   F   **8.** Messages conveying neutral information to the receiver should use the direct plan.

T   F   **9.** Not all positive messages should be organized by using the direct plan.

T   F   **10.** Confidentiality of information is a necessity with some inquiries

Multiple Choice

In the blank at the left, write the letter that represents the best answer.

_____   **1.** Positive information is emphasized most by
             a. a single-sentence paragraph near the middle of the letter.
             b. a single-sentence paragraph at the beginning of the letter.

     c. a two-sentence paragraph at the beginning of the letter.

     d. a two-sentence paragraph at the end of the letter.

_____ **2.** Which of the following is NOT considered an appropriate subject for an inquiry message?
     a. Complaints
     b. Individuals
     c. Products
     d. Services

_____ **3.** Which statement would be a good opening for a letter approving an adjustment?
     a. Your letter about the broken chairs arrived Monday.
     b. Your replacement chairs will be shipped today.
     c. Because your continued business is important to us, we examined your claim.
     d. I am pleased to inform you that your chairs were shipped today.

_____ **4.** Which is NOT a characteristic of a positive information opening in a direct plan?
     a. Stresses writer's interests
     b. Is positive
     c. Provides related explanation
     d. Uses emphasis techniques

_____ **5.** Which statement would be the most appropriate close for an adjustment message?
     a. We regret the inconvenience that this has caused you.
     b. Hopefully, our corrective action will keep this situation from happening again.
     c. Best wishes on your store expansion.
     d. This problem will never reoccur.

Matching

Write the letter of the best answer in the blank preceding the term. Some answers may be used more than once; others may not be used at all.

_____ **1.** Announcement of an unscheduled pay increase

_____ **2.** Claim letter

_____ **3.** Content development

_____ **4.** Direct plan

_____ **5.** Explanation

_____ **6.** Friendly close

_____ **7.** Inquiry

_____ **8.** Opening

_____ **9.** Request approvals

_____ **10.** Sales appeal

a. expresses appreciation

b. you–viewpoint

c. use only when appropriate

d. presents related information

e. letter of appreciation

f. done after situation is analyzed

g. used for positive and neutral messages

h. normally given

i. should de-emphasize the inconvenience that sender has experienced

j. appears before the explanation

k. used to obtain information

l. type of unsolicited positive message

Completion

Complete each item by writing the necessary word or words.

1. A well-constructed explanation should stress the benefits to the _____ instead of the interests of the _____.

2. Positive and neutral messages should be organized by using the _____ plan.

3. A direct plan should be used for messages presenting _____, _____, or _____.

4. The sales appeal, if appropriate, should follow the _____.

5. An effectively written positive or neutral message integrates _____ _____ into the direct plan.

6. Immediate information is provided to the receiver by identifying the order or request in the _____ paragraph or a _____ line.

7. The direct plan begins by presenting _____.

8. An individual's rights may be protected in an inquiry when _____ and _____.

9. Adjustments to claims should be made _____.

10. The content of the message is developed using the direct plan after the _____ and _____.

Review Questions

1. What is an adjustment message? How is its content organized?

2. How can the you–viewpoint be implemented in a positive information message?

3. Explain the differences between writing a positive information message to an employee and writing a positive information message to a customer.

4. What must take place in the message development process before the content is developed?

5. Explain why the following paragraph would be weak in opening an inquiry message.

   Your company has an excellent reputation in the business community. Your products are being used throughout the United States.

CASE PROBLEMS

Inquiries

1. Twelve employees of Brenham National Bank will be in Dallas, Texas, from May 29 to June 2. They have expressed an interest in either arriving one day early or leaving one day late so that they may attend the LaCosta Dinner Theater. You have been selected by the group to plan this activity. Write a letter to LaCosta to obtain details. Supply necessary information to make it a complete letter.

2. Carefree Insurance is concerned about the physical condition of its employees. After surveying the employees, it was decided that providing a racquetball court would be the best facility for getting its employees into shape. You have been assigned to gather information about constructing a racquetball court. Write a letter to Sports Freaks, Inc., to obtain this information. You will need enough information for management to make a decision.

3. You would like to put vinyl siding on your home, and you are considering installing it yourself. You need information such as cost, available styles and colors, installation procedures, and warranty. Write a letter to Quality All-Season Siding to obtain this information. Supply necessary information to make it a complete letter.

Requests

4. You are vice president of your college's Future Business Leaders student organization. One of your responsibilities is to coordinate the organization's public service activities within your community.

   Jeremy Cole is organizing the Special Olympics for the region. He has asked your organization to provide seven members to assist in judging events. Future Business Leaders normally does not commit itself to activities that are not directly related to business; however, the Special Olympics is very important to the community and your organization will receive excellent exposure. You believe your organization should participate in this activity. Write Mr. Cole a letter expressing appreciation for being considered to participate in such worthwhile event. Tell him that you will have seven individuals there and can assist with more persons if necessary.

5. You are the owner of Useful Robotics. Your organization manufactures robots that are sold or leased to business firms to perform repetitive and monotonous chores.

   The Forney Community Theater is presenting a comedy in which a robot is used. The director of the theater has requested that your organization donate the use of a robot. The theater group has a very limited budget and cannot afford to buy or lease one.

   Prepare a letter to the director, Ms. Amy Ragan, and tell her that a robot will be provided. This gesture will give your company much-needed publicity for its product. Be sure to include any necessary details to make this a complete request approval.

6. Because of your business education background, a local church has asked you to audit its books for the past year. The set of books is small and will not take too much time.

   Write Reverend Jim Wright a letter accepting this responsibility. In this letter you need to establish a date when you could meet with the church treasurer to go over the books.

Claims

7. You ordered a food processor from Kitchen Accessories after seeing one demonstrated on television. Unfortunately, the processor does not work nearly as well as the one demonstrated on television. The first time you sliced vegetables with it, the blade bent. Write Kitchen Accessories asking for a full refund. Add the necessary facts to make your letter complete.

8. Steven Erwin has always been overweight. He recently went to Pounds Away Camp to lose weight. This camp is especially designed for individuals who want to lose weight while vacationing.

   After two weeks at the camp, Steven gained four pounds instead of losing weight. When Steven returned home, he remembered that the camp guaranteed a weight loss.

   Write a letter for Steven requesting a refund of $1,800 (the cost of his camping vacation). Indicate that a copy of the brochure advertising the guaranteed weight loss is included.

9. Pat Freeman's home on the edge of town looks beautiful, with four large young trees in the front yard. The trees were 15 feet tall when planted last fall. Westrup's Nursery did an excellent landscaping job with the trees.

   Pat is unhappy now after a winter snowstorm broke three of the main limbs from one of the trees. Write a letter for Pat to Westrup's Nursery and ask for a $575 refund or a replacement tree. The storm was not so severe that the trees should have been damaged.

Adjustments

10. The Pounds Away Camp is operated for people who would like to lose weight while vacationing. You have been operating this camp for six years and have seen hundreds of people lose weight. Because of this experience, you began issuing guarantees that would give any person who did not successfully lose some weight a full refund.

    Steven Erwin stayed at the camp for two weeks and gained four pounds. Although it was rumored that Steven was snacking at night (which is against the rules), your staff did not catch him. Because you have a reputation to maintain, you will give him a full refund of $1,800. Write him a letter approving the adjustment; enclose the check.

11. You operate Fantasia Ceiling Fans, a mail-order business. Priscilla Young of Jackson, Mississippi, purchased a 60-inch, contemporary ceiling fan from you this past summer. You have just received a letter from her stating:

    I purchased a 60-inch, limited edition, polished brass fan with four white blades in late June. Your advertisement stated that it was constructed of sturdy, die-cast zinc and steel. It contained a 3-speed reversible fan motor.

    The fan was installed by a licensed electrician the first week in July. During Labor Day weekend I heard an unusual sound when I turned on the fan. Over the next two weeks as I was using the fan, the noise seemed to get worse. Now the fan is vibrating whenever I turn it on. I wish you would send me a new fan or refund my money.

    Write Ms. Young a letter explaining that you will send her a new fan. In this letter tell her that apparently the motor is malfunctioning. Inform her that the new fan will have the same warranty as the original fan. Add necessary details.

12. Ralph Teague is the customer service representative for Alvarado Electronics, a manufacturer of sound and video equipment. Equipment manufactured by Alvarado Electronics is sold in retail stores throughout the United States.

    Jane Mayfield has written a letter to Ralph stating that she purchased one of Alvarado's tape recorders 14 months ago from a local discount store. The recorder was guaranteed for one year. She would like a replacement unit since the warranty had so recently expired.

    Write a letter for Mr. Teague telling Ms. Mayfield that she can return the tape recorder to any store that sells Alvarado products. The letter should explain that the store is to give Ms. Mayfield a replacement unit and then forward the defective recorder to Alvarado Electronics for reimbursement.

Unsolicited Positive and Neutral Messages

13. Champion Savings has expanded its facilities during remodeling. It added an activity room that can be used for various functions, such as bridal showers, birthday parties, anniversaries, receptions, etc. The room is available to any of Champion's patrons who have both checking and savings accounts with the institution. Write a form letter that could be sent to all of Champion Savings customers.

14. As vice-president of advertising for Safety Tire Company, you are aware of the advantages of high-volume sales. To achieve these high-volume sales, you realize that rewards must be given to retailers.

    A program has been developed by Safety Tire Company that will give the retailer a rebate of $35 for every ten tires sold during a six-month promotional period. Write a letter informing the retailers of this promotional plan. Add the necessary facts to make your letter complete.

15. Yuki Yamaguchi has been working as an information-processing operator for Cummins Insurance for the past three months and has developed excellent work skills.

    You are the human resources manager for Cummins. Write a memo to Yuki promoting her to supervisor of the Information Processing Service Center. Explain to her that you normally do not promote anyone in your organization that quickly, but you are doing so in this situation because of her outstanding performance.

CHAPTER 7

Goodwill
Messages

LEARNING ACTIVITIES

True or False?

Circle T if the statement is true; circle F if the statement is false.

T   F   **1.** The writer of a letter of condolence should empathize with the sorrow of the situation.

T   F   **2.** Sympathy messages should be written in the indirect approach because they deal with negative material.

T   F   **3.** Rarely should you use a handwritten message for a letter of condolence.

T   F   **4.** It is acceptable for an invitation to be printed on company stationery.

T   F   **5.** A goodwill message should cause the receiver to form a positive opinion of the sender.

T   F   **6.** An invitation need not contain suggested dress or the place that the function will be held if an RSVP is requested because the receiver will be contacting the sender before the function.

T   F   **7.** It is acceptable for the sender to write a personal note on a printed holiday greeting card sent by a company.

T   F   **8.** Goodwill messages are important in building positive relationships.

T   F   **9.** Welcome letters should not contain any coupons or sales offers.

T   F   **10.** When sending any goodwill letter, an informal letter will be more effective than a formal letter.

Multiple Choice

In the blank at the left, write the letter that represents the best answer.

_____ 1. A formal, typewritten letter is most appropriate for
   a. a condolence letter.
   b. an invitation.
   c. a welcome letter.
   d. a holiday greeting.

_____ 2. Which of the following approaches would be the best method to use in constructing a letter of condolence?
   a. Convey sympathy, give necessary details, and close apologetically.
   b. Offer assistance, express sympathy, and close positively.
   c. Express sympathy, recall details of tragedy, and close apologetically.
   d. Express condolence, offer assistance, and refer to the future.

_____ 3. The most appropriate method of preparing an invitation for a social function with a guest list of several hundred people is
   a. a formal typewritten letter.
   b. an informal typewritten card.
   c. a handwritten note.
   d. a printed card.

_____ 4. Which of the following is the best beginning sentence for a letter of appreciation?
   a. You have worked for our company for more than 35 years.
   b. You are invited to attend our annual banquet on August 22.
   c. Thank you for serving as a judge for the Outstanding Citizen of the Decade contest.
   d. We know that you will enjoy your retirement.

_____ 5. One consideration for the formality of a goodwill message is
   a. the amount of money you have to spend.
   b. how well you know the receiver.
   c. the importance of the message.
   d. the educational level of the receiver.

Completion

Complete each item by writing the necessary word or words.

1. Congratulatory messages should be written using the _____ approach.

2. The most personal and appreciated condolence messages are _____ .

3. Messages of sympathy should be closed by _____ .

4. Letters of appreciation may be sent for _____ or for
_____ .

5. Necessary details of an invitation include:

   a. _____

   b. _____

   c. _____

   d. _____

6. Some companies send distinctively designed holiday greeting cards that contain their
   _____ and _____.

7. A welcome message may be sent to _____,
   _____, or _____.

8. A goodwill message is written to communicate _____ and
   _____.

9. A _____ is a request for an individual's presence.

10. The most preferred method of accepting a new credit card customer is to send a
    _____ letter.

Review Questions

1. Cite three situations that are appropriate for a letter of condolence.

2. Briefly discuss the composition of a condolence message.

3. Compare the contents of an invitation to the contents of a welcome message.

4. When is it appropriate to send each of the following forms of messages—handwritten, typewritten, or printed?

WORD PUZZLE

Across

3. Determined by how well you know the receiver

4. Important when sending goodwill messages

5. Commercially produced and sent in place of typed letter

8. _____ Greetings

9. Message sent for a one-time favor

10. _____ messages build good relationships

11. Letter used to familiarize customer with the company

Down

1. Messages sent for accomplishments

2. Approach used in goodwill messages

6. Message of sympathy

7. Request for a reply to an invitation

CASE PROBLEMS

Congratulations

1. Derek Martin was transferred to your company's branch office in Dallas, Texas, 10 years ago. Since his arrival in Dallas, he has been trying to get accepted into the Dallas Symphony. Last week he was accepted. Write a complete letter to Derek congratulating him on his accomplishment.

2. Hog Barn has been operating three restaurants in Missouri. The company has just announced an expansion of its operation to a five-state area. You are the loan officer for the Rolla State Bank. Write a letter to Darryl Gipson, president of Hog Barn, congratulating him on the expansion. Add any necessary details to make this a complete letter.

3. One of your high school classmates has been elected president of the Student Government Association at the school she attends. This position is quite prestigious since the school has more than 15,000 students. Prepare a letter of congratulations for the accomplishment. Add necessary details.

Condolence

4. Green Bottle Manufacturing was hit by a tornado that destroyed its building. Fortunately, the tornado occurred at night and no one was injured. Assume that you are manager of Swain's Realty and have a vacant building that you would like to make available to Green Bottle. Write a condolence letter to Green Bottle and add information to make it a complete letter.

5. Casi, the daughter of Cyndi Gomez, a systems analyst for your company, was killed yesterday in an accident involving a drunk driver. Write a letter to Mr. and Mrs. Gomez expressing your sympathy.

6. Heidi Wisehart started a small business in your community last year and was doing quite well. About three months ago the economy slowed down, causing financial problems for Ms. Wisehart. Last week her business declared bankruptcy. It seems to you that the bankruptcy was caused by the economic slowdown and not by poor management on the part of Ms. Wisehart. Write her a letter of condolence adding necessary details.

Appreciation

7. You are the scoutmaster for Post 442 in Reston, Virginia. You invited Houston Nutt to give the charge (motivational speech) to the scouts at an awards ceremony. He gave an outstanding presentation. Write a letter thanking him for this act of courtesy.

8. You chaired a regional Special Olympics in your community. You would like to send a letter to each of the volunteers who made the event successful. Write a personalized form letter that could be sent. Details should be added to the letter to make it complete.

9. You have just completed serving as state president of a professional organization. You would like to send thank-you letters to the individuals who served on the board of directors during your term of office. Compose a letter that would be personalized but still could be sent to everyone on the board.

Invitation

10. You are a junior partner in a local CPA firm which has recently hired two new CPAs. You and your spouse would like to have them and their guests to an informal dinner at your home. Write this invitation, including necessary details, such as time, date, and directions to your home.

11. The band in your school is having its annual pancake breakfast. Write a form letter that could be sent to the businesspersons in your community inviting them to this annual fund-raiser. Include all the details that the message receivers would need.

12. Your community is opening a new youth recreational center. The facility will provide activities for ages 4 through 18. Write a form letter that can be personalized and sent to all area residents inviting them to the open house.

Holiday Greeting

13. Lambert's Insurance Brokers is sponsoring a Valentine Dinner and Dance for its employees and their guests. As the human resources manager, prepare a memo that could be sent to the employees. The memo should contain an RSVP so that adequate food can be ordered.

14. Capital Investments has leased Water World, a water recreational park, for July 3. You are the human resources manager for the company. Write a memo wishing all employees a happy Fourth of July and inviting them and their families to Water World. Add any necessary details to make this a complete message.

15. The Tender Steak House would like to provide a free Thanksgiving dinner to all senior citizens in your community. It feels that the best method of inviting the senior citizens for the holiday treat is to have a letter appear in the local newspaper. Write a letter that could be printed in your local newspaper.

Welcome

16. You are the president of Panorama Shores Homeowners' Association. Each month the association holds a block party for the residents of the subdivision. Write a letter welcoming new residents to the neighborhood and inviting them to attend the next block party. Add necessary details.

17. You are the president of the Student Government Association and would like to welcome all freshmen to your campus. The school administration has furnished you with a list of these individuals. Prepare a letter that could be sent to these freshmen.

18. Morgan and Gunn is a large accounting firm that hires interns from colleges and universities. As personnel director for the firm, you are responsible for welcoming new employees. Write a personalized form letter to be sent to the new interns, welcoming them to the firm. Remember that the company usually hires the outstanding interns after they earn their degrees.

CHAPTER 8

Negative Messages

LEARNING ACTIVITIES

True or False?

Circle T if the statement is true; circle F if the statement is false.

T F **1.** The indirect plan should be used for all negative messages.

T F **2.** An advantage of using the indirect plan for negative messages is that after giving the negative information, the logical explanation is presented and offsets the message's negative impact.

T F **3.** It is possible to write a negative message showing how your refusal actually benefits your receiver.

T F **4.** In the opening buffer of a negative message, the sender tries to maintain neutrality and not imply either a yes or a no.

T F **5.** The logical explanation section of a negative message contains a helpful alternative solution.

T F **6.** The logical explanation justifies the negative information.

T F **7.** It is a good technique to de-emphasize the negative information by placing the refusal or unfavorable news in a dependent clause.

T F **8.** If appropriate, you can give an additional reason in the constructive follow-up, justifying the unfavorable news.

T F **9.** The off-the-subject close should contain a sincere apology to help build goodwill with the receiver.

T F **10.** The concept of the indirect plan can be applied to most negative message situations.

Matching

In the blank at the left, write the letter of the part of the indirect plan that best fits each requirement listed.

_____ 1. Introduces the explanation

_____ 2. Provides alternative solution

_____ 3. Presents convincing reasoning

_____ 4. Says what can be done
(not what cannot)

_____ 5. Stresses receiver interests
and benefits

_____ 6. Maintains neutrality

_____ 7. Telegraphs explanation

_____ 8. Stays off negative subject

_____ 9. Follows logical explanation

_____ 10. Follows opening

a. The opening buffer

b. The logical explanation

c. The negative information

d. The constructive follow-up

e. The friendly close

Multiple Choice

In the blank at the left, write the letter that represents the best answer.

_____ 1. The overall strategy for most negative messages is
   a. the direct plan.
   b. the persuasive plan.
   c. the indirect plan.
   d. the goodwill plan.

_____ 2. An important requirement of the opening buffer in the indirect plan is that it
   a. presents convincing reasoning.
   b. provides coherence.
   c. follows the logical explanation.
   d. says what can be done.

_____ 3. In the logical explanation section of the indirect plan, it is most important to
   a. keep the content as brief as possible.
   b. show how the negative information benefits your receiver.
   c. use mostly positive words.
   d. keep off the subject.

4. If you cannot provide an alternative solution in a negative message, in the constructive follow-up you are encouraged to
  a. give additional reasoning.
  b. be positive.
  c. personalize it.
  d. be optimistic.

5. The negative information in a message should
  a. be given quickly.
  b. follow the opening.
  c. present convincing reasoning.
  d. introduce the explanation.

6. In the friendly close of a negative message, it is best to
  a. maintain neutrality.
  b. provide convincing reasoning.
  c. say what can be done.
  d. be warm and optimistic.

7. The direct plan should be used for negative information when
  a. goodwill is important.
  b. the receiver should read the logical explanation first.
  c. an apology is important.
  d. your receiver prefers that the negative information be given first.

8. Which of the following statements is not an advantage of the indirect plan?
  a. It emphasizes the negative information.
  b. It permits reason to prevail.
  c. It changes a negative situation to a positive one.
  d. It maintains a calm approach.

9. Of the following, which is the most effective phrasing for negative information?
  a. I am sorry to refuse your request for a refund for the microwave oven.
  b. Our policy does not permit refunds in cases like this.
  c. Rather than a refund, we will be glad to provide instruction on the operation of the oven.
  d. While we realize you are not completely satisfied with the microwave oven, we do believe that you can be with additional training.

10. The best opening for an adjustment refusal is
  a. I am sorry . . .
  b. Your complaint has been received, and . . .
  c. Thank you for your letter of . . .
  d. Your letter requesting an adjustment has been received, and . . .

WORD PUZZLE

Across

1. Request _____

5. Good plan for negative messages

8. _____ refusal message

10. Common negative word

11. Letter that handles a large number of refusals

12. Negative information is bad _____ to receiver

13. Buffer

14. Nature of the explanation

17. Information that needs to be de-emphasized

18. Opening _____

Down

1. _____ refusal

2. _____ close

3. _____ goodwill

4. Avoid these words

6. Use this plan when appropriate

7. Give negative information _____ in direct plan

8. Same wavelength

9. Important to maintain

15. The opposite of bad

16. _____-the-subject closing

CASE PROBLEMS

Request Refusals

1. Write a request refusal letter to the chair of the nominating committee of your community service club who has asked that you serve as president next year. You have been a member of the club for five years, and you think its purposes are worthy, but you are not in a position now to take a leadership role. You simply do not have the time. You have just been promoted to supervisor and are working between 50 and 70 hours per week and see no change in your work requirements in the foreseeable future. Supply any additional details needed.

2. You manage a restaurant in the Shade-Tree Mall. You have a moderate amount of window space where you display a copy of your menu. Juan Ramirez, a local banker who is also chairperson of the mental health board, has written to you requesting permission to place a large placard in your window space. The placard is promoting a worthwhile cause—the annual Marathon for Mental Health. Your policy, however, is to display only your menu in the limited window space. Supplying any additional necessary details, write Mr. Ramirez, giving him the negative information. It will be important to justify your policy in your letter.

3. One of the employees in your plant, Sandra Smith, is running for mayor of your city. If she wins the election, she will take a leave of absence to serve her term. You have agreed to this. Also, as is your policy, you have contributed $500 to each of the two candidates in the election. You believe in assisting all sides in getting their positions before the voting public. Ms. Smith has just sent you a memo requesting a second $500 contribution. In this request, as in her first request, she very persuasively points out that it will be in your company's interest that she win the election. Write her the necessary request refusal message. Show her how your policy is in her best interest and benefits her most. As a suggested alternative, you could offer permission to both candidates for them to solicit contributions through memos to the employees.

Adjustment Refusals

4. As adjustment manager of the retail mail-order company that sells "Young Jeans," you have received a challenging claim letter. David Robinson writes, "I have just laundered the jeans I purchased from you last week. They shrank, they faded, and they wrinkled! Send my $49.95 back today, and tell me what to do with the jeans." You must refuse his claim. All the things that he said happened undoubtedly did. In fact, the small brochure attached to each pair of these all-cotton jeans said they would. Write Mr. Robinson an adjustment refusal that will stress the qualities of "Young Jeans" that will serve him well. In fact, you will not only turn down his claim, but you will also try to sell him (in your suggested alternative) some "Just You Jeans" that will not shrink, fade, or wrinkle.

5. You manage Swimmers' Delight, a discount, mail-order bathing suit sales organization. Write a form letter to customers who are asking to return bathing suits purchased from your company. Your policy—stated clearly in your sales catalog—is not to allow the return of bathing suits for personal hygiene reasons. In all your catalogs you stress that customers should select sizes carefully. You provide a sizing chart and fabric samples to assist them in their suit selections. Be sure to justify your policy to your customers. Add any necessary details to make this a complete form letter that fully utilizes the indirect plan for negative messages.

6. Joanna Collins has just left your office. She is upset. The new car she purchased from your dealership is having carburetor problems. She has called you several times about the problem. She wants the

problem corrected at no cost to her. Each time you have tried to explain patiently (a) that her warranty expired a month before the trouble began, and (b) that you can repair the carburetor if she will leave the car in your garage for two days. Joanna is so angry now she is threatening to sue. You believe she has no legal basis for her position, but you do not want to be sued or to lose any future business you might have with her. You feel the best thing to do at this point is to write her an adjustment refusal letter, clearly specifying the situation. You have also decided, as a suggested alternative, to offer to do the necessary repair at cost. Write the indirect letter that will restore Joanna's goodwill.

Credit Refusals

7. As credit manager for Hahn's, Inc., you review applications for store credit cards. Today's mail brought an application from a newly married male. He is requesting that he and his wife be extended a line of credit and that credit cards be issued to each. A check of their credit ratings reveals that he currently is in bankruptcy, but that her credit rating is good. Write a credit refusal to him, but try to keep his and his wife's business.

8. You are the credit manager for Rosewood Wholesale Electric in Chicago, Illinois. An application for credit has just been received from Parkdale Electric, Parkdale, Illinois, a relatively new cash customer. With the application, Parkdale provided all the necessary supporting references, none of which look good. Although Parkdale's cash purchases are getting larger each month (last month they were a gratifying $903), the references indicate a poor Dun and Bradstreet rating, a poor assets-to-liabilities ratio, and evidences of slow payment from the Chicago Credit Bureau report. Using the indirect plan, deny Parkdale Electric credit, but retain its business. In the near future Parkdale may qualify for credit with you; in the meantime, you definitely want its cash business. Add the facts necessary to make your letter complete in proper format.

9. Write a form letter that can be sent to older persons who have applied for your new "BuyFree" credit card but who do not meet your credit requirements. It is ironic that many of these older people are quite well off financially; but because they have always paid cash for their purchases, they have not established creditworthy records. Refuse to issue the credit card in so tactful a manner that you are sure to get their business when they take the necessary steps to establish their credit records. In fact, do more than is expected by telling them some of the steps they can take to establish a credit record— for example, borrowing a small amount from a bank and paying it back before it is due, buying an item on credit from a local retailer and paying promptly for it, etc. Add any necessary details.

Unsolicited Negative Messages

10. When you accepted your present position as manager of accounting services eight months ago, you thought you would stay in the position at least three years. But now you have had an excellent offer from a rival accounting firm to manage one of its branch offices. Not only will you have more responsibility, but you will also receive a significant increase in pay. It is a major advancement for you. You know, however, that your superior will be seriously disappointed, perhaps even angry, for she thought you would remain with the firm for at least another three to five years. Write an indirect plan letter that explains your decision. State the negative information positively. In the suggested alternative section of the letter, speak of your assistant's ability to assume your position.

11. Write an unsolicited form letter to the students in a dormitory telling them that their old, favorite dorm is going to be razed at the end of the semester and that they will have to move to another dorm or to private housing. The dorm is no longer cost-effective to maintain and only marginally meets safety and health standards. In addition, a parking lot is desperately needed for student parking in the area where the old dorm is located. After your opening buffer and explanation, do more than is expected and tell them how your office will facilitate their selection of new housing and their move to it.

12. You have talked to Mary Cohoon on three separate occasions about her unsatisfactory performance as a salesperson for the Harrison Insurance Agency's Salina office. The situation is getting worse instead of better. You have decided that the only decision left is to let her go. She obviously does not have the aptitude for sales work. She, too, is very unhappy with her performance. She has tried hard to sell insurance, but has had limited success. Write Mary a compassionate, unsolicited negative memo in which you terminate her employment with the Harrison Insurance Agency. There are definite receiver benefits in this dismissal situation. An employer does a favor for unsatisfactory employees, at least in part, by dismissing them when their skills do not match the job requirements.

CHAPTER 9

Persuasive
Messages

LEARNING ACTIVITIES

True or False?

Circle T if the statement is true; circle F if the statement is false.

T F **1.** Persuasive messages are seldom used for internal communication.

T F **2.** Persuasive messages normally should be presented using the indirect approach.

T F **3.** Mechanical devices, such as color, should not be used to gain the reader's attention in a persuasive message because they distract the reader.

T F **4.** Emphasizing benefits to the receiver will help diminish negative reactions that the receiver may have to taking the desired action.

T F **5.** Both simple and complex requests are used by business organizations.

T F **6.** Recommendations should be written using the indirect plan.

T F **7.** Often a salutation is omitted in a sales letter.

T F **8.** To maintain an honest reputation, you should mention your product's weaknesses to the customer.

T F **9.** The appeal stage of collection messages is used for customers who simply forgot to make a payment.

T F **10.** The number of steps in each collection stage should be consistent from customer to customer to ensure unbiased treatment.

Multiple Choice

In the blank at the left, write the letter that represents the best answer.

_____ 1. Which of the following is NOT a correct statement about the attention part of the indirect plan?
   a. It should be short.
   b. It should be positive.
   c. It should be given immediately.
   d. It should discuss benefits to the receiver.

_____ 2. Which of the following methods of getting the receiver to take action should NOT be used in persuasive requests or sales letters?
   a. Using threats
   b. Offering free prizes
   c. Offering coupons
   d. Giving a deadline

_____ 3. The indirect plan should be used for
   a. routine claims.
   b. goodwill messages.
   c. recommendation letters.
   d. adjustment grant letters.

_____ 4. Which of the following comments best describes a collection message in the appeal stage?
   a. Is a reminder for a customer who forgot to pay
   b. Uses the indirect persuasive outline
   c. Is written from the writer's point of view
   d. Is not concerned with customer goodwill

_____ 5. Which of the following sentence beginnings best asks for action in a collection appeal stage?
   a. You must send . . .
   b. I appeal to you to . . .
   c. Please send . . .
   d. I expect your . . .

Matching

Write the letter of the best answer in the blank preceding the term. Some answers may be used more than once; others may not be used at all.

_____ 1. Action section

_____ 2. Attention section

_____ 3. Desire section

_____ 4. Interest section

_____ 5. Past due

_____ 6. Collection messages

_____ 7. Recommendations

_____ 8. Sales messages

_____ 9. Special claims

_____ 10. Warning stage

a. begins most persuasive messages

b. ends most persuasive messages

c. submitted on all organizational levels

d. builds on attention

e. uses direct plan

f. written in three stages

g. organized using both direct and indirect plan

h. example of message in reminder stage

i. provides proof of receiver's benefits

j. other than routine

k. frequently omits salutation

Completion

Complete each item by writing the necessary word or words.

1. The two primary purposes of a persuasive message are

   _____ and

   _____.

2. Messages that are considered persuasive are:

   a. _____

   b. _____

   c. _____

   d. _____

   e. _____

   f. _____

3. The final paragraph of a persuasive message is designed to get the reader to

   _____.

4. Describing _____ to the receiver will create interest in the receiver.

5. _____ are submitted at all organizational levels.

6. Special claims requiring persuasion should be written using the _____ plan.

7. As you compose a sales message, you should emphasize the _____ and omit mentioning _____.

8. The three stages of collection messages are _____, _____, and _____.

9. The customer needs to be analyzed carefully before a collection letter is written in the _____ stage.

10. The indirect plan is used for collection letters in the _____ stage.

Review Questions

1. What advantage is gained by using the indirect plan instead of the direct plan for persuasive messages?

2. Explain the indirect plan that should be used for persuasive messages in business communications. Include all parts of the plan in your explanation.

3. Compare the organizational plans for the two types of requests that an organization uses.

4. Identify five techniques that may be used in sales messages to gain the reader's attention.

5. Compare the appeal stage of collection messages to the warning stage.

CASE PROBLEMS

Persuasive Requests

1. Turner Properties owns a storage facility that rents spaces for short-term and long-term periods. Space may be rented on a monthly or annual basis. Turner Properties has decided to increase the rent beginning next month. The current and new rental fees are:

| | Current | | New | |
	Monthly	Annual	Monthly	Annual
5′ × 5′	$9.50	$95.00	$11.50	$115.00
5′ × 10′	$18.00	$180.00	$23.00	$230.00
10′ × 10′	$35.00	$350.00	$47.00	$470.00
10′ × 20′	$70.00	$700.00	$95.00	$950.00

In addition to providing storage, the facility provides an on-site manager; security fence; garage-style, roll-up doors; and 24-hour availability. Prepare a form message that can be sent to current renters informing them of the rental increase and encouraging them to accept the increase. Add necessary details.

2. Jack Page has been an active supporter of several youth organizations in your community. Project Leadership has decided to honor Jack for his contribution by naming him recipient of this year's Citizen of the Year Award. As president of Project Leadership, it is your responsibility to get Jack to the banquet without letting him know that he is to receive the award. Add details to make the letter complete.

3. You are chairperson of the program committee for Westwood Sports Club. One of your college class-mates, Pat Evans, was a member of the U.S. Olympic team and won a silver medal in marksmanship. You did not know her well but would like to invite her to your club to give a demonstration. Pat charges a fee for her demonstration, however, and your club has no money. Write her a letter persuading her to give this demonstration without charge. Add necessary facts to make the letter complete.

Recommendations

4. The bookstore at your school handles a limited line of clothing in addition to textbooks. The line of clothing that it carries is of excellent quality, but it is very expensive. Write a letter to the bookstore manager recommending that the present items be replaced with more affordable clothes.

5. You are president of Students for Action (SFA). This organization supported the present governor during the recent election. SFA would now like Art Fowler, an alumnus of your college, to be appointed to the state education board. Art has maintained his interest in your school's activities and has been very successful in operating a hardware store since his graduation. He is active in three civic organizations. Art would be an excellent individual to have on the board. Write a letter to the governor recommending Art for the position. Add necessary details to make the letter complete.

6. You are the manager of a horse farm in Lexington, Kentucky. Angela Forrester has been your veterinarian for 10 years. She has done an excellent job with the horses on your farm. Angela would like to become the veterinarian for the Commonwealth of Kentucky. Write a letter to the governor recommending her for the position.

Special Claims

7. Jane Broach purchased a fur coat on sale from Helene's Furrier for $2,150. She has had the coat for only one year, and the fur has started falling out. Jane has asked you to write a letter to Helene's requesting either a refund or another coat. Write the letter adding any details to make the letter complete.

8. Last summer you purchased a new motor home that you plan to use during vacations, weekends, and holidays. You started noticing minor problems (loose seat braces, leaking faucets, leaking side windows, tears in the seams of three seats, and several rattles) in the motor home after you had owned it for only three months. On your last trip with the motor home, the engine sputtered for most of the trip. On your return, you took it to the repair shop, where you learned that the carburetor needs replacing. You are unhappy with the motor home and feel that it is a "lemon." Write to Hughes Homes, the manufacturer, asking for a replacement motor home. Add details to make the letter complete.

9. During a recent hailstorm, damage was done to the roof of your home. An adjustor awarded you full damages, less your $100 deductible. Two weeks later, your television had to be repaired. The repair service representative stated that the damage was due to lightning, and the only storm in the past month was the one that damaged your roof. Write a letter to the insurance company requesting that the $135 repair bill for the television be combined with the roof so that you do not have to pay the $100 deductible twice. Add any details to make the letter complete.

Sales Messages

10. You are the owner-manager of a sporting goods store that is sponsoring a fishing derby; proceeds will go to Abused Children. Registration fees (not tax deductible) for the event are $10. Ten prizes totaling $500 will be awarded. Write a letter to customers on your mailing list announcing this derby.

11. Harbor Hills Marine is a full-service boat company. Recently, it began selling jet skis for water-sport recreation. The jet skis are similar to snowmobiles but are made to ride on water. They are dependable and provide the owner with years of fun and excitement. Prepare a sales message that could be sent to residents within the county. Add details to make the letter interesting and realistic.

12. Apple Motors is a sports car dealer. It has made arrangements with a local bank to finance all new cars sold to students who are within three months of graduation. Write a letter that could be sent to seniors notifying them of this arrangement.

Collection Messages

13. Fred's Photography specializes in wedding portraits. Fred's requires a $100 deposit and 25 percent of the balance when the pictures are delivered. The remaining balance can then be paid over a six-month period. Mark and Janet Slatta had a June wedding and received their pictures the first week of July, paying 25 percent at that time. However, they have not made a payment on the balance since getting the pictures. It is now November, and the balance is still $475.25. Fred's has written six collection letters without getting a response. Write a letter for Fred's informing Mark and Janet that they have until December 1 to pay the $475.25 or the account will be given to an attorney. Add details to make the letter complete.

14. You deliver the local newspaper to earn money for school. The newspaper requires that carriers pay their bill for each month by the fifth of the following month. Alan Taylor, a subscriber, has not paid his bill for the last three months. You have enclosed four reminders with his paper, but they did not obtain a response. Write a letter to Alan appealing for the $22.50 due and explain why it is important that you collect his money each month. You do not want to antagonize Alan and lose him as a customer.

15. Northside Fitness Center is a diverse health facility. It provides its members with a full court gymnasium, outdoor pool and tennis courts, exercise classes, indoor running track, supervised weight training, racquetball courts, and child care during certain hours. A reminder sticker is pasted to overdue bills. Most members will respond to the reminders, but some members need more persuasion in order to pay their bills. Prepare a form letter that could be sent to members who are two or more months behind in their monthly dues. Add details to make the letter complete.

CHAPTER 10

The Job Search and Resume

LEARNING ACTIVITIES

True or False?

Circle T if the statement is true; circle F if the statement is false.

T   F   **1.** The first step in a job campaign is to find positions for which you can apply.

T   F   **2.** Solicited positions are positions that are available but are unlisted or unadvertised.

T   F   **3.** The most valuable source of information about jobs will likely be your career center.

T   F   **4.** One of the common services of your career center is the maintenance of credentials files for candidates.

T   F   **5.** Newspaper advertisements are a good source of information only about jobs in a given geographical area.

T   F   **6.** With the advent of the Internet, you now have a new method for seeking your career position and making worthwhile connections.

T   F   **7.** State governments provide employment services.

T   F   **8.** Since you are the product you are selling in your job search, you will want your resume to contain only positive information.

T   F   **9.** In analyzing your qualifications, the most important facts to list are evidences of your accomplishments.

T   F   **10.** A targeted resume is less powerful than a general resume.

T   F   **11.** Most employers prefer the functional resume format over the reverse chronological resume format.

T   F   **12.** The education section should always follow the resume opening.

T   F   **13.** If your high school record is fairly recent and shows considerable accomplishment, include it in your resume; otherwise, omit it.

T   F   **14.** Keywords are verbs that label you; it is best to have around 20–25 keywords for a scannable resume.

T   F   **15.** You are encouraged to provide full information on your references, including their business telephone numbers.

Multiple Choice

In the blank at the left, write the letter that represents the best answer.

_____ **1.** Which of the following employment services does NOT provide information about jobs in the private sector?
    a. Career Center
    b. State government employment office
    c. Federal government employment office
    d. Private employment agency

_____ **2.** Parallelism in a resume means
    a. starting all material at the left margin.
    b. using the same part of speech to start a series of items.
    c. having complete sentences for the narrative resume content.
    d. giving the same amount of space to each section.

_____ **3.** Most employers prefer the
    a. targeted, reverse chronological resume.
    b. targeted, functional resume.
    c. general, reverse chronological resume.
    d. general, functional resume.

_____ **4.** The best arrangement for a resume for a college graduate who has extensive experience is
    a. opening, references, education, references.
    b. opening, education, experience, references.
    c. opening, experience, education, references.
    d. opening, experience, references, education.

_____ **5.** The primary purpose of a resume is to
    a. summarize information about you.
    b. prepare you for completing an application form.
    c. communicate clearly your strengths and weaknesses.
    d. obtain a job interview.

_____ **6.** The purpose of keywords is to
    a. enable managers to determine if you match their openings.
    b. correctly and honestly describe you and your qualifications.
    c. mark an electronic trail for your employment.
    d. All of the above.

_____ **7.** Which of the following parts of an Education section in a resume is the most important?
   a. Courses
   b. Organization memberships
   c. Achievements
   d. Dates of attendance

_____ **8.** Which of the following is the general recommendation on including reference data in a resume?
   a. Do not provide reference data.
   b. Provide complete reference data.
   c. Indicate that references are available on request.
   d. Indicate that references are on file in college placement office.

_____ **9.** For new college graduates with limited experience, the preferred number of pages for a resume is
   a. one.
   b. two.
   c. three.
   d. the number needed to cover essential information.

_____ **10.** Employment laws
   a. prohibit a job applicant from revealing his or her gender.
   b. permit a job applicant to reveal his or her race.
   c. permit an employer to ask for the name of an applicant's religion.
   d. prohibit an employer from asking for the name of an applicant's college.

Matching

Write the letter of the best answer in the blank preceding the description. Some answers may be used more than once; others may not be used at all.

_____ 1. Advertised or listed positions

_____ 2. Listing of qualifications

_____ 3. Optional section

_____ 4. Presents information by

_____ 5. Unadvertised positions

_____ 6. Job information source

_____ 7. Resume purpose

_____ 8. Presents most recent information first

_____ 9. Nontraditional resume

_____ 10. Critical resume content

a. unsolicited positions

b. personal information

c. reverse chronological resume

d. career center

e. interviewer

f. solicited positions

g. obtain job interview

h. accomplishments

i. resume

j. reference

k. functional resume

Completion

Complete each item by writing the necessary word or words.

1. Your most important business communication will be about your _____.

2. The most helpful publication available at a career center is the _____.

3. Two major services of many career centers are
   _____ and
   _____.

4. The primary purpose of private employment agencies is to _____
   _____.

5. State government employment agencies list employment opportunities both
   _____
   _____.

6. In your job campaign, _____ are the product you are selling.

7. In analyzing your qualifications, four helpful categories are:

   a. _____

   b. _____

   c. _____

   d. _____

8. The primary purpose of a resume, along with an application letter, is _____
   _____.

9. The _____ can be developed on your computer and
   then uploaded to your own home page on the Web.

10. It is best to have around _____ keywords for a scannable resume.

WORD PUZZLE

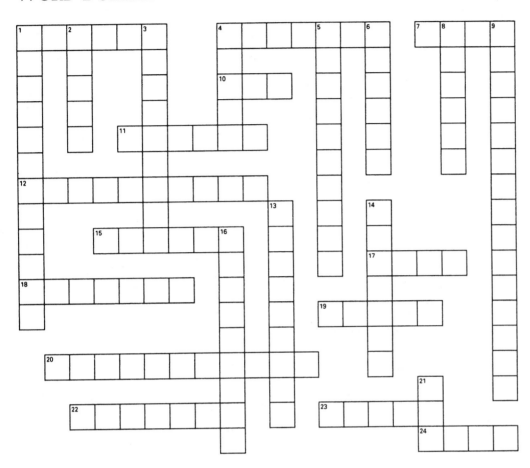

Across

1. Summary of qualifications
4. Not personalized
7. Personal _____ sheet
10. Source of jobs
11. _____ objective
12. Work
15. Type of achievement
17. Synonymous with *resume*
18. Special abilities
19. Minimum number of references
20. Unadvertised
22. _____ employment agency
23. Don't include with resume
24. Paper color for resume

Down

1. Job _____
2. A special capability
3. Training
4. _____ point average
5. Should be favorable
6. Solicited jobs are _____
8. Evidences of achievements
9. Achievements, learning, contributions
13. Unpaid employment
14. Not chronological order
16. Advertised
21. Position

CHAPTER 11

Employment Communication and Interviewing

LEARNING ACTIVITIES

True or False?

Circle T if the statement is true; circle F if the statement is false.

T   F   **1.** Application letters are sales letters—with you as the product.

T   F   **2.** You can combine a targeted resume and a general application letter.

T   F   **3.** The primary purpose of an application letter is to get the job.

T   F   **4.** You can be quite creative in the attention-getting opening of an application letter.

T   F   **5.** You should indicate how you meet the employer's job requirements in an application letter.

T   F   **6.** All application letters are sometimes called cover letters.

T   F   **7.** The most important part of an application letter is the section in which the writer tries to convince the employer that he or she fits the job.

·T   F   **8.** As an interviewee, you should have some key questions of your own for the interviewer.

T   F   **9.** When asked in an interview what salary you would expect, the best answer is, "I am open on the salary question."

T   F   **10.** The amount of appropriate eye contact with interviewers is 25 percent of the time, and possibly less, depending on their cultural backgrounds.

T   F   **11.** In accepting an interview invitation, suggest how busy you are by indicating it is somewhat difficult for you to schedule a time for the interview.

T   F   **12.** Even if you are definitely not interested in the job, it is still appropriate to follow up an interview.

T   F   **13.** If you think it has been too long since you have heard about your application with an employer, it is appropriate to call or write.

T   F   **14.** The Web is not a good source for learning about a company.

T   F   **15.** When resigning from a job, you should use the direct plan of communicating.

Multiple Choice

In the blank at the left, write the letter that represents the best answer.

_____ **1.** An application letter should be written following the guidelines for
  a. neutral messages.
  b. persuasive messages.
  c. goodwill messages.
  d. negative messages.

_____ **2.** The most important part of an application letter is the
  a. attention-getting opening.
  b. summary of qualifications.
  c. action-promoting close.
  d. logical explanation.

_____ **3.** An application letter is your opportunity to
  a. show how you fit the job.
  b. impress the reader with your communication ability.
  c. transmit your acceptance of a job interview.
  d. convince the reader that he or she should give you the job.

_____ **4.** In the close of an application letter, the way to get an interview is to
  a. plead for it.
  b. ask directly for it.
  c. imply that you want it.
  d. not push it.

_____ **5.** If you have a number of appointments and commitments during the next few weeks, in the close of an application letter discussing a possible interview time, you should
  a. mention that your schedule is not completely free.
  b. briefly and generally list your major appointments and commitments.
  c. say that hopefully your schedules will match.
  d. offer to be at the interviewer's office at his or her convenience.

_____ **6.** For most employers, the final decision on whether to offer a job will be based on the
  a. application letter.
  b. resume.
  c. interview.
  d. follow-up communication.

7. Your preparation to interview begins
_____
   a. when you start a job campaign.
   b. after the analysis of your qualifications.
   c. after you have prepared your resume.
   d. when an interview invitation is received.

8. Examples of questions you should acquire about the organizations are
_____
   a. the size of the organization or company.
   b. the geographic locations of the company.
   c. the type of service or products that the company offers.
   d. All of the above.

9. Appropriate behavior during an interview does NOT include
_____
   a. being assertive.
   b. being vague.
   c. being calm.
   d. talking positively about other employers.

10. Following up an interview
_____
   a. is inappropriate.
   b. should be done with a phone call.
   c. should be done with a letter.
   d. should be done in person.

Completion

Complete each item by writing the necessary word or words.

1. The three major parts of a well-designed application letter are:

   a. _____

   b. _____

   c. _____

2. In the opening of an application letter, the two most important things to do are:

   a. _____

   b. _____

3. The three most important things to do in the middle section of an application letter are:

   a. _____

   b. _____

   c. _____

4. In the close of an application letter, the candidate should:

   a. _____

   b. _____

   c. _____

5. In preparation for an interview, you should prepare yourself to answer the question, "What salary do you expect in this job?" Two good sources of information about salaries being paid for similar jobs are _____ and
    _____.

6. The signals an interviewer may give you that an interview is ending are _____
    _____.

7. If an interviewer challenges you by asking difficult questions or by appearing disinterested or even irritated, you should _____.

8. After an interview, the candidate should _____
    _____.

9. Thorough research of a company before an interview with help you in two basic ways:
    _____ and
    _____.

10. When you have accepted an employment offer and have completed a successful job campaign, it is important to _____
    _____.

APPLICATION EXERCISES

1. Write the first sentence of an application letter for a job as an advertising copywriter for a public relations firm.

2. Write the last sentence for an application letter in which you are seeking an interview.

3. In an interview, what answer would you give to a first question similar to the following: "Why should we hire you for this position?"

4. Write the sentence in a resignation letter in which you give your employer the specific news that you are resigning.

5. A letter accepting employment is a positive communication and should use the direct plan. What kind of information should be included in each of the three paragraphs.

6. You have been offered two managerial positions by comparable companies. You have decided to accept the offer from the company that pays more and that is located closer to your family. How would you phrase the key rejection part of the letter in which you turn down the other company's offer?

7. Write the first sentence in a thank-you letter you are sending to the four persons who agreed to serve as your references in your recent successful job campaign.

WORD PUZZLE

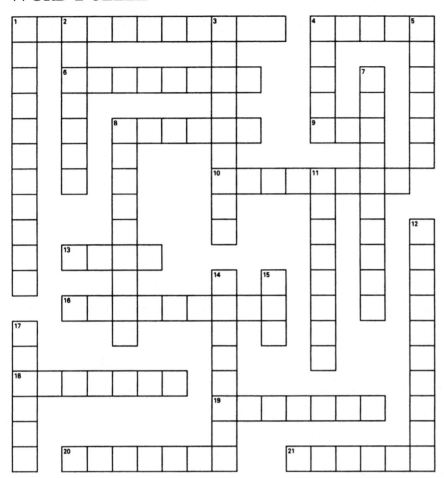

Across

1. Request for employment
4. _____ confidence
6. Check quality of interview
8. Job worth
9. Your qualifications should _____ the job requirements
10. Not direct
13. _____ attention in opening
16. Be ready to answer _____
18. Abstract of qualifications
19. Include for reference
20. Create
21. Quit

Down

1. Ask _____ questions
2. _____ for an interview
3. Meeting with potential employer
4. Length of application letter
5. Opposite of indirect
7. Plan ahead
8. Advertised
11. _____ the company
12. Request to come to an interview
14. Purpose of application letter is to _____ employer to read resume
15. _____ directly for interview
17. Application letter and _____ are the application packet

CHAPTER 12

Research Techniques and Proposals

LEARNING ACTIVITIES

True or False?

Circle T if the statement is true; circle F if the statement is false.

T   F   **1.** The first task in the planning step in conducting research is to define the scope of the study.

T   F   **2.** The Gantt chart is an effective way to show the budget for a business study.

T   F   **3.** Secondary sources of information include individuals, company files, and observations.

T   F   **4.** Primary information is published information gathered from company, public, or college libraries.

T   F   **5.** The least costly survey technique is the mail survey.

T   F   **6.** Web online questionnaires are becoming an accepted method of collecting data.

T   F   **7.** Managers should avoid using informal observation to obtain information because it is not a scientific technique.

T   F   **8.** To analyze data means to look at the parts by comparing and contrasting them.

T   F   **9.** A conclusion is a recommendation.

T   F   **10.** Business proposals should be viewed by writers as persuasive messages.

T   F   **11.** The most important, and probably the largest, section in most proposals is the benefits section.

T   F   **12.** The proposal summary section tells which parts are included in the proposal, but it should not try to tell what the content is in those parts.

T   F   **13.** When responding to an RFP, be sure to provide all information requested, even if you do not feel that something is helpful to your proposal.

T   F   **14.** A good way to present the description-of-the-solution section in a business proposal is to relate the content to each of the benefits listed earlier in the proposal.

T   F   **15.** Every proposal will have an evaluation plan.

Multiple Choice

In the blank at the left, write the letter that represents the best answer.

_____ **1.** Which of the following is the best statement of a problem for a business study?
  a. How can we find out the best methods for processing account payments?
  b. A study to process account payments more effectively.
  c. To determine the most effective method for processing account payments.
  d. To study the most effective methods to process account payments.

_____ **2.** The best way to limit the scope of a study is to
  a. select factors that will be studied.
  b. set a budget limit that will not be exceeded.
  c. establish a commitment to a time schedule.
  d. agree with your manager on a problem statement.

_____ **3.** The survey question that will yield the most comparable and useful information is the
  a. open-ended question.
  b. leading question.
  c. interview question.
  d. forced-answer question.

_____ **4.** Recommendations in a business study should follow from the
  a. findings.
  b. analysis.
  c. conclusions.
  d. benefits.

_____ **5.** Which of the following statements about business studies is the LEAST true?
  a. They are required infrequently in business.
  b. They are conducted to provide solutions.
  c. They are a common business activity.
  d. They are limited in scope.

_____ **6.** The most important proposal element in the following list is the
  a. proposal summary.
  b. description of the proposed solution.
  c. problem or need.
  d. evaluation plan.

_____ **7.** If the proposal solution is implemented, the outcomes to be realized are most likely to appear in what section of a proposal?
   a. Purpose
   b. Problem or need
   c. Benefits of the proposal
   d. Background

_____ **8.** The best description of business proposals from a proposal writer's viewpoint is that they are
   a. certainties.
   b. requirements.
   c. responsibilities.
   d. opportunities.

_____ **9.** Which of the following should NOT be placed in an appendix to a business proposal?
   a. Product specifications
   b. Organization's history
   c. Description of the solution
   d. Qualifications of personnel

_____ **10.** The best approach for writing a long, complex proposal is
   a. a team of writers.
   b. a team of writers with a team of readers giving feedback.
   c. an individual writer with a team of readers giving feedback.
   d. a team of writers with an individual writer providing coherence.

Matching

Write the letter of the best answer in the blank preceding the description. Some answers may be used more than once; others may not be used at all.

_____ 1. Third step in a study

_____ 2. Study boundaries

_____ 3. Cost estimate

_____ 4. Mail survey

_____ 5. Personal interview

_____ 6. Periodical

_____ 7. Leading question

_____ 8. Analysis summary

_____ 9. Published material

_____ 10. Gantt chart

_____ 11. Request for proposal

_____ 12. Recommendation

_____ 13. Cover letter or memo

_____ 14. Name of proposal, receiver, submitter, etc.

_____ 15. Lists contents

_____ 16. Proposal in capsule form

_____ 17. Definition of terms

_____ 18. Supporting materials

_____ 19. Reference list

_____ 20. Way to judge success

a. appendix

b. bibliography

c. budget

d. conclusion

e. study solution

f. evaluation plan

g. glossary

h. influence readers

i. high-response survey

j. least costly survey

k. objective

l. analysis

m. primary information

n. RFP

o. time schedule

p. secondary information

q. limits of the study

r. proposal summary

s. table of contents

t. title page

u. transmittal message

Completion

Complete each item by writing the necessary word or words.

1. Once the appropriate subject is identified, a further in-depth search can be completed using a
   _____.

2. A clear, accurate, written _____ of a study can serve as an agreement about what is to be studied.

3. The boundaries of a study are determined by:

   a. _____

   b. _____

   c. _____

4. When searching on the Web, one can begin with a subject index, which is a
   _____ of subject indexes.

5. A helpful technique in searching for the published materials available on a given topic is a
   _____.

6. The basic ways to survey people are:

   a. _____

   b. _____

   c. _____

7. The two basic types of survey questions are _____
   and _____.

8. The three basic ways to obtain primary information are _____,
   _____, and _____.

9. In solicited proposals, the elements to be included in the proposal are often specified in the
   _____.

10. A proposal is an analysis of a _____and a recommendation for a
    _____.

11. Proposals initiated by an individual or an organization that are not in response to an RFP are
    _____.

12. The two primary roles of the purpose statement in a proposal are to help the reader understand
    _____ and
    _____.

13. The benefits of the proposal represent the_____of the implementation of the proposed solution.

14. The evaluation plan in a proposal is a way to judge the _____ achieved if the proposal was implemented.

15. A very popular example of a subject index is _____.

Review Questions

1. Name the five steps in conducting a research project.

2. Describe how to develop a clear, accurate, written statement of the problem for a study.

3. Explain how a subject index and search engines are used on the Web.

4. Define what drawing conclusions and making recommendations mean.

5. Briefly describe the four ways proposals can be categorized.

6. List the qualities of successful proposals.

7. What are the common proposal elements?

8. What should the purpose of the proposal contain?

9. What does "the benefits of the proposal must be in you–viewpoint" mean?

10. Describe the nature of the proposal element called "the description of the proposed solution."

APPLICATION EXERCISES

1. Interview three students in your business communication class to determine what they think are the five most valuable things they have learned from your course thus far. Organize your findings so that you can analyze them. Determine the differences and the similarities and draw conclusions. List your conclusions.

2. List five factors you think appropriate to study for solving the following problem: Should school be dismissed on the Tuesday of election day.

3. Analyze the following data, draw conclusions, and make a recommendation.

   Number of employees who want a flextime work schedule: 67 of 100

   Number of employees who want to come in early and leave early: 34

   Number of employees who want to work the regular schedule: 33

   Number of employees who want to come in late and work late: 33

4. Write a proposal to your employer making a case for a four-day work week.

5. List the benefits that you would include in a proposal that employees and their families be provided free health insurance as a part of their fringe-benefit program.

6. Based on your experience with the service of a retail store (fast food restaurant, department store, sporting goods store, or other retail store), write a suitable proposal for improved service that could be given to the store manager.

CHAPTER 13

Report Preparation

LEARNING ACTIVITIES

True or False?

Circle T if the statement is true; circle F if the statement is false.

T   F   **1.** An executive summary, if used, appears in the body of a formal report.

T   F   **2.** Progress reports provide managers with statistical information at regularly scheduled intervals.

T   F   **3.** The inverted pyramid format used for news releases begins with a summary.

T   F   **4.** Information obtained from secondary sources and used in formal reports must be footnoted, but footnoting is optional in informal reports.

T   F   **5.** The conclusions section presents statistical comparisons of the findings.

T   F   **6.** An executive summary of a multipage report is normally no longer than two pages.

T   F   **7.** The scope defines the boundaries of the study.

T   F   **8.** The formal report is used less in business than is the informal report.

T   F   **9.** Pages in the supplementary section should be numbered by placing small roman numerals at the bottom of each page.

T   F   **10.** The appendix contains items directly related to the study but excluded from the body to improve readability.

Multiple Choice

In the blank at the left, write the letter that represents the best answer.

_____ 1. Which of the following is normally NOT included in a footnote?
   a. Complete name of author
   b. Volume of publication
   c. City in which published
   d. Publishing company

_____ 2. Which of the following is NOT a division of a formal report?
   a. Preliminary
   b. Body
   c. Appendix
   d. Supplementary

_____ 3. Which two parts may be combined in some formal reports?
   a. Letter of authorization and letter of transmittal
   b. Conclusions and recommendations
   c. Glossary and bibliography
   d. Procedures and findings

_____ 4. Which of the following is NOT true about news releases?
   a. If more than one page, -more- should be printed at the bottom of each page.
   b. Contact person's name and phone number should be shown on news release.
   c. It should be double-spaced.
   d. It should contain a conclusion.

_____ 5. Which of the following is NOT a common use for letter reports?
   a. Submitting an annual report
   b. Presenting information
   c. Giving recommendations
   d. Reporting statistical data

Completion

Complete each item by writing the necessary word or words.

1. The two types of written reports are _____ and _____.

2. The cover for a written report should contain _____ and _____.

3. The _____ indicates why the study was conducted.

4. Preliminary pages should be numbered using _____ numerals, and the body should be numbered with _____ numerals.

5. A report's _____ and _____ should be indicated in the report title.

6. Terms that are defined in a formal report should be included in a _____.

7. The _____ clearly identifies the specific situation researched.

8. A short report used to communicate routine information within an organization is a _____.

9. A news release should end with a _____ or a _____.

10. A technical report is used to communicate _____ _____ information.

Review Questions

1. Describe the purpose of policy statements and discuss how they are used in business organizations.

2. List and describe the body parts of a formal report.

3. List and describe the supplementary parts of a formal report.

4. Compare a progress report with a periodic report.

APPLICATION EXERCISES

1. A professional organization in your area of study has awarded you a four-year scholarship. One requirement for continuation of the scholarship is that you submit an annual report to the organization's scholarship committee giving details of the progress you have made during the past year. Write a report giving these details for the most recent year. Include in the report your educational plans for completing your degree.

2. Your local Industrial Foundation has hired you for the summer to prepare a report on the quality of the school system in your city. This report will be given to companies considering a move to your city. The report must include all levels of education in the area. Gather the facts and write a formal report that could be used to convince businesses to move to your city.

3. A student organization on your campus is initiating new members. It would like to honor the initiates with an article in the local newspaper. Write a news release for the organization.

WORD PUZZLE

Across

3. May be combined with recommendations

6. Abstract

9. Published at regularly scheduled intervals

12. Dots in table of contents

13. Boundaries of study

14. Comparison of findings

15. Report of significant changes

Down

1. Company guidelines

2. Definitions

4. Contains indirectly related material

5. References

7. Official record of meeting

8. News

10. Main section of report

11. External report

CASE PROBLEMS

1. Americana Collectibles currently does not use telecommunication in its operations. As a new employee of the company, prepare a report for upper management outlining the enormous use of telecommunication equipment in businesses throughout the United States. Present the data given below in the best form to convince management that Americana needs to expand into telecommunication.

	Telecommunication Equipment	
Year	Total Dollars Spent	Number of Companies Using Equipment
1998 (est.)	$1,145,800,000	12,330,175
1997	790,555,600	10,525,850
1996	420,883,793	7,190,335
1995	303,520,175	5,840,287
1994	193,645,200	4,210,495

2. Scenic Vacations is a travel agency that is expanding to provide charter trips for groups. These charter trips would be for one, two, or three days. Scenic has two options for providing these charter trips: (1) pay a flat rate for the use of buses from a bus company, or (2) purchase its own buses and hire its own drivers.

   In the first option, Scenic would pay $1.05 a mile to rent the buses from a bus company. The bus company would provide the driver and the bus.

   In option 2, Scenic would purchase a bus for $195,000 and hire its own driver. A driver can be hired for $0.34 a mile and $20 a day for meals. The driver would be provided with $50 a day for a room on overnight trips. Scenic would have an annual insurance cost of $30,000 and fuel and maintenance costs of $0.52 a mile.

   Prepare a report that could be sent to Scenic Vacations' owner, Terry Carpenter, recommending the option that should be selected. Include in the report a plan for charging groups that use the travel agency for their excursions.

3. You have been asked to speak at an Honors Seminar on gender equity in business publications. You analyze by gender the number of articles accepted for publication in professional business journals. Use the results of your investigation (shown on the next page) to prepare a report that could be presented to each participant.

Publication	Year	Number of Articles	Author	
			Male	Female
A	1998	74	67	48
	1997	72	71	59
	1996	75	62	60
	1995	65	51	47
B	1998	80	45	59
	1997	82	54	53
	1996	81	51	62
	1995	80	42	58
C	1998	68	50	63
	1997	73	59	60
	1996	70	62	54
	1995	69	65	46

CHAPTER 14

Graphic Aids

LEARNING ACTIVITIES

True or False?

Circle T if the statement is true; circle F if the statement is false.

T F **1.** A graphic aid is any illustration used to aid the reader in understanding the text material and to shorten the written text.

T F **2.** All graphic aids within a written report should be identified by an appropriate title.

T F **3.** Art images saved on a diskette for later importation into a word processing document are called *clip art.*

T F **4.** A source note should be used whenever content for an illustration is obtained from another source.

T F **5.** A pie chart should never contain only one exploded segment.

T F **6.** Temporary positions within an organization are shown on an organization chart with broken or dotted lines.

T F **7.** A line graph is the best illustration for showing trends in quantitative data over a period of time.

T F **8.** The data being illustrated determines the interval between each vertical and horizontal line on a line graph.

T F **9.** When used as a graphic aid, a map should never be larger than five inches in size.

T F **10.** Drawings emphasize differences in statistical data.

Multiple Choice

In the blank at the left, write the letter that represents the best answer.

_____ 1. Which of the following statements about source notes is correct?
  a. The word *source* should be followed by a semicolon.
  b. The source note is placed above the illustration.
  c. Only items originated by the report writer require a source note.
  d. The word *source* normally consists of all uppercase letters.

_____ 2. The best graphic aid to illustrate how the parts of a whole are distributed is the
  a. organization chart.
  b. pie chart.
  c. stacked bar graph.
  d. drawing.

_____ 3. A positive-negative bar graph
  a. shows plus or minus deviations from a fixed reference point.
  b. shows changes over a period of time.
  c. shows changes in more than one value at a time.
  d. shows differences in values within variables.

_____ 4. Which of the following methods would be least likely to deceive the reader of a report?
  a. Having different-sized images in a pictograph
  b. Beginning a bar graph at 100,000
  c. Having bars in a bar graph represent every five years
  d. Omitting some of the nonessential details in a drawing

_____ 5. Which of the following statements about graphic aids is NOT correct?
  a. Illustrations must be titled.
  b. A graphic aid should appear prior to the text describing it.
  c. Graphic aids should be numbered consecutively.
  d. Titles may be placed above or below the illustration.

Completion

Complete each item by writing the necessary word or words.

1. Any illustration used to assist a reader in understanding the text material is a

   _____.

2. Illustrations that indirectly relate to the written text should be placed

   _____.

3. _____ are used whenever content for an illustration is obtained from another source.

4. Tables are printed displays of words and numbers arranged in _____ and

   _____.

5. _____ illustrate relationships among departments and personnel within
   the departments.

6. _____ positions are connected by broken or dotted lines in an
   organization chart.

7. A _____ chart may have a segment exploded to emphasize the segment.

8. A _____ graph shows differences in values within variables.

9. The two types of line graphs are _____ and

   _____.

10. A personal touch can be added to a business report by including a

    _____.

Review Questions

1. When and how should illustrations obtained from other sources be identified?

2. Explain why a drawing may be an effective graphic aid for illustrating a complicated idea or
   procedure.

3. Discuss the appropriate use for each of the five variations of bar graphs.

WORD PUZZLE

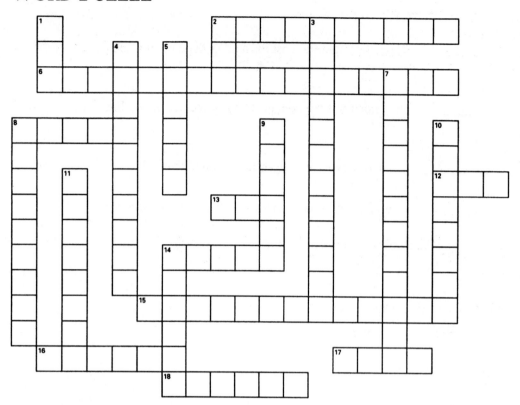

Across

2. Adds personal touch

6. Graph that shows deviations from a fixed reference point

8. Flow _____

12. Clip _____

13. Graphs that may be simple, broken, or stacked

14. Data presented in rows and columns

15. Pie chart shows _____

16. Used to identify lines in a graph

17. Graph that shows changes over a period of time

18. Line graph showing one value

Down

1. Shows geographic relationships

2. Chart showing how parts relate to one another

3. Chart showing lines of authority

4. Uses images of items

5. _____ bar graph

7. Graphic aid

8. Direction in which pieces of pie chart are displayed

9. _____ note

10. Omit clutter and emphasize desired details

11. Line graph showing changes in more than one value at a time

14. Line graphs illustrate _____

APPLICATION EXERCISES

1. Construct the most appropriate graphic aid to show the comparison of sales to expenses for Classic Boots in the past five years.

Year	Sales	Expenses
1995	$432,300	$274,000
1996	415,000	261,300
1997	633,700	315,250
1998	595,500	310,760
1999	903,100	429,875

2. The following data show how a student could spend his or her day. Construct a graphic aid that most effectively illustrates how each activity compares with the other activities.

In class	3 hr 30 min
Studying	4 hr 15 min
Eating	1 hr 45 min
Resting	6 hr 45 min
Entertainment	3 hr 45 min
Working	4 hr 0 min

3. Teri's Auto Supply conducted sales throughout the year at different percentage reductions. Records were kept to correlate the percentage of sales discount with the total amount of sales. Using the following figures, construct a graphic aid that illustrates the comparisons most effectively.

Amount of Reduction	Amount of Sales
10%	$ 8,450
20%	15,100
30%	19,300
40%	23,250
50%	25,775
60%	13,425

4. Benton School keeps records of its sports-related injuries that require medical attention. Construct a graphic aid that best illustrates the number of injuries within individual sports for each of the past five years.

Year	Basketball	Football	Soccer	Track
1998	1	19	0	3
1997	2	26	1	1
1996	2	20	0	4
1995	3	31	2	2
1994	1	27	1	1

5. Estimate your personal expenses for a period of one month. Use a graphic aid to illustrate the distribution of the expenses.

CHAPTER 15

Listening and Nonverbal Messages

LEARNING ACTIVITIES

True or False?

Circle T if the statement is true; circle F if the statement is false.

T   F   **1.** A listener who associates meanings with stimuli will be more successful in recalling information at a later time.

T   F   **2.** People normally can hear at a faster rate than they can speak.

T   F   **3.** A speaker's message should be evaluated after he or she has completed the entire presentation.

T   F   **4.** A speaker may volunteer more information if you give negative feedback.

T   F   **5.** A speaker should not display facial expressions because they may change the meaning of an oral message.

T   F   **6.** Forming a rebuttal to the material presented will help you concentrate on the speaker's presentation.

T   F   **7.** Your physical appearance may affect how other people perceive your oral message.

T   F   **8.** For a salesperson to show confidence in his or her product, the salesperson should squeeze the customer's hand as tightly as possible during a handshake.

T   F   **9.** Nonverbal communication may transmit an unintentional message.

T   F   **10.** An individual glancing around the room while speaking indicates an interest in the surrounding room and the subject of the message.

Multiple Choice

In the blank at the left, write the letter that represents the best answer.

_____ 1. Which is NOT a mode commonly used to listen to messages?
  a. Cautious listening
  b. Careful listening
  c. Skimming
  d. Scanning

_____ 2. The mental filters assign meaning to stimuli during which stage?
  a. Filtering
  b. Hearing
  c. Visualizing
  d. Interpreting

_____ 3. Which of the following is NOT an effective guideline for listening?
  a. Keep an open mind.
  b. Use feedback.
  c. Maximize notetaking.
  d. Stop talking.

_____ 4. Which of the following is NOT a speech characteristic that may be a barrier to listening?
  a. Tone
  b. Unusual pronunciation
  c. Volume
  d. Dialect

_____ 5. Which of the following is true about nonverbal communication?
  a. Communication is improved if the employee is sitting and the boss is standing.
  b. The message transmitted by physical appearance will depend on the occasion.
  c. Messages conveyed through body language follow no observable patterns.
  d. A person who is late transmits the message of being busy and, therefore, important.

Completion

Complete each item by writing the necessary word or words.

1. The listening process consists of the following:

  a. _____

  b. _____

  c. _____

  d. _____

2. The three modes of listening are _____,
_____, and _____.

3. The _____ mode is the least careful type of listening.

4. Daydreaming is a _____ distraction.

5. Dialects, jargon, unusual pronunciations, and speech impairments are _____ barriers.

6. One of the best ways of gaining information is through effective _____ _____.

7. Types of nonverbal communication are

    a. _____

    b. _____

    c. _____

    d. _____

8. Manner of dress communicates a _____ message.

9. A type of nonverbal communication that depends on the proximity to the person in charge is _____.

10. Smiles and frowns are forms of _____ language.

Review Questions

1. Describe the differences between hearing and listening.

2. Why is it important for a good listener to know the purpose of the message?

3. How can effective listening improve your communication?

4. Describe several forms of body language and explain how each transmits a nonverbal message.

APPLICATION EXERCISES

1. Observe how space is allocated on your campus. Include office and parking spaces. Write a short report analyzing your observations.

2. Analyze a local, state, or national figure according to speech characteristics and nonverbal communication. Be prepared to demonstrate these nonverbal actions to see if the class can guess who is being portrayed.

3. Observe young children, young adults, and elderly adults at a common gathering. Record the nonverbal messages that each group presents. Describe the messages that are transmitted.

4. Record the nonverbal messages that several instructors in your school transmit. Bring the list, without the instructors' names, to class and discuss with the class the meanings associated with each message. Do any of the meanings distract from the instructors' presentations?

WORD PUZZLE

Across

1. Least careful mode of listening

4. Mode of listening for general concepts

7. Assigning meaning to stimuli

9. Stimulation of auditory nerves by sound waves

11. Form of body language

Down

2. Listening is an _____ process

3. A speech characteristic barrier

5. Eliminates unwanted stimuli

6. A type of nonverbal communication

8. Remembering at a later time

10. Includes the size of a physical area

CHAPTER 16

Oral Communication Essentials

LEARNING ACTIVITIES

True or False?

Circle T if the statement is true; circle F if the statement is false.

T   F   **1.** Lower-level managers spend more time in oral communication than do higher-level managers.

T   F   **2.** A speaker can relax his or her sound-producing organs with two or three deep breaths.

T   F   **3.** It is possible to indicate comparisons and contrasts with voice pitch.

T   F   **4.** While voice pitch can be used effectively for emphasis, voice volume refers simply to being heard by others.

T   F   **5.** It is important to talk slower during large-group presentations than during conversations.

T   F   **6.** The way in which you join sounds to say a word is called *enunciation*.

T   F   **7.** Having unrealistic expectations for an oral communication can have a negative effect on confidence.

T   F   **8.** Selecting two or three gestures and using them throughout a presentation will help relieve nervousness.

T   F   **9.** Never admit you've forgotten someone's name; the conversation will help you remember who the person is.

T   F   **10.** Anticipating what the other person will say will help you be a lively conversationalist.

Multiple Choice

In the blank to the left, write the letter that represents the best answer.

_____ 1. Pitch refers to the
   a. highness or lowness of your voice.
   b. strength of your voice
   c. timbre of your voice.
   d. volume of your voice.

_____ 2. To avoid a monotone voice, you should vary your
   a. pitch and speed.
   b. pitch and volume.
   c. pitch, volume, and speed.
   d. volume and speed.

_____ 3. If you exhibit too little confidence when speaking to others, they will
   a. feel discomfort.
   b. feel negative toward you.
   c. reject you.
   d. reject your message.

_____ 4. A good way to gain confidence when speaking to a group is to
   a. concentrate on yourself and how you sound.
   b. keep the emphasis on the listeners and use the you–viewpoint.
   c. picture the audience dressed in underwear.
   d. tell yourself that you can do it.

_____ 5. The best way to convey sincerity is to
   a. avoid humor.
   b. smile.
   c. speak slowly.
   d. use a tone of importance.

_____ 6. To have comfortable eye contact with an audience, you should try to look
   a. at the foreheads of the group members
   b. into the eyes of every member of the group.
   c. into the eyes of selected members of the group.
   d. slightly above the heads of the group members.

_____ 7. Gestures should be
   a. carefully designed.
   b. contrived.
   c. natural.
   d. repetitious.

_____ 8. True feelings are best communicated by
   a. eye contact.
   b. facial expressions.
   c. posture.
   d. words.

_____ **9.** The correct volume level during an oral presentation is loud enough
   a. for everyone in your audience to hear you.
   b. for your average listener to hear you.
   c. to be heard by those who are interested.
   d. to convey strength.

_____ **10.** The best guide for face-to-face conversations is to be appropriately
   a. aggressive.
   b. aloof.
   c. angry.
   d. assertive.

Completion

1. Your _____ consists of your _____ and bearing.

2. Project enthusiasm by speaking with _____ and _____.

3. Your oral communication effectiveness will depend on the _____ of your voice and the _____ of your presence.

4. When you try to inhale deeply in preparation for speaking, the air should go all the way to the _____.

5. Pitch refers to the _____ or _____ of the voice.

6. _____ your receiver will help you maintain a _____ manner during telephone conversations.

7. An _____-ended question promotes dialogue.

8. Too little or too much confidence are both caused by _____.

9. The five stages of a conversation are _____, _____, _____, _____, and _____.

10. When speaking with an angry customer, first deal with _____, then handle the _____.

Matching

Write the letter of the best answer in the blank preceding the description. Some answers may be used more than once; others may not be used at all.

_____ 1. First stage in the conversation process

_____ 2. Raw material for speaking

_____ 3. Sufficient to be heard

_____ 4. Excite an audience with

_____ 5. Gain credibility with

_____ 6. Convey true feelings

_____ 7. Way messages sound

_____ 8. Cordial conclusion to a conversation

_____ 9. Says "I like you"

_____10. Join sounds to say a word

a. air

b. appearance

c. closing

d. enthusiasm

e. enunciate

f. facial expressions

g. gestures

h. greeting

i. know-it-all-attitude

j. opening

k. pronounce

l. sincerity

m. smile

n. summary

o. tone

p. volume

Word Search

Fill in the blanks. Then locate and circle the words in the puzzle. Words may be displayed horizontally, vertically, or diagonally.

1. A _____ helps to create a warm, friendly environment.

2. A presentation to a large group is also called a _____.

3. A _____ presentation is an example of collaborative oral communication.

4. _____ contact varies with culture.

5. The _____ *t*'s are tight tongue, tight jaw, and tight lips.

6. A speaker's voice should never be _____.

7. When a speaker's voice rises at the end of a sentence, he or she sounds _____.

8. To avoid damaging your vocal cords, find and use your natural _____.

9. To create a mood of sorrow or seriousness, _____ the volume of your voice.

10. Speakers should work to achieve a _____ between speed and clarity.

11. A person's most important possession is his or her _____.

12. If possible, answer your phone on the _____ ring.

13. Avoid telephone _____.

14. Be prepared to have your calls answered by a _____ _____ system.

15. Correct _____ will improve your appearance and give you a feeling of confidence.

s	b	a	l	a	n	c	e	y	l	e	n	t
f	m	l	t	a	v	o	i	e	n	a	a	s
t	r	o	u	b	l	e	s	o	m	e	m	r
e	a	s	w	e	n	g	d	e	x	c	o	l
n	e	g	o	f	y	o	r	e	p	f	n	o
t	l	v	o	i	c	e	m	a	i	l	o	w
a	i	t	s	r	i	f	u	r	t	e	b	e
t	m	i	t	s	y	t	s	h	c	n	n	p
i	s	p	h	c	e	e	p	s	h	a	a	v
v	l	o	w	e	r	u	t	s	o	p	l	o
e	n	o	t	o	n	o	m	c	h	n	a	m

CHAPTER 17

Oral Communication Applications

LEARNING ACTIVITIES

True or False?

Circle T if the statement is true; circle F if the statement is false.

T   F   **1.** The first item of business at each meeting of a small group should be to determine the agenda.

T   F   **2.** A leader should never resolve a group conflict simply by moving to the next agenda item because he or she believes the conflict isn't worth the group's time.

T   F   **3.** Each participant in a group meeting should assume responsibility for encouraging appropriate participation by all members.

T   F   **4.** An impromptu oral presentation is one that is delivered without time to prepare.

T   F   **5.** The size of the group to which you speak determines whether you conduct an audience analysis.

T   F   **6.** A good way to share the text of your presentation with your audience is to display it as a visual aid.

T   F   **7.** The overall organizational framework for a presentation is (1) opening, (2) body, and (3) closing.

T   F   **8.** Even practiced, professional speakers can experience nervousness before a presentation.

T   F   **9.** Question-and-answer sessions can be used to enhance a speaker's relationship with his or her audience.

T   F   **10.** The moderator of a question-and-answer session facilitates the process but never asks a question.

Multiple Choice

In the blank to the left, write the letter of the best response.

_____ 1. The quality of thinking that emerges from small-group meetings
  a. has no relationship to what one person can achieve alone.
  b. is usually higher than one person can achieve alone.
  c. is usually lower than one person can achieve alone.
  d. is usually the same as what one person can achieve alone.

_____ 2. Which of the following techniques is NOT helpful when trying to resolve group conflicts?
  a. Postpone the discussion to give time for reflection.
  b. Reflect the group feeling of frustration by being firm.
  c. Seek a compromise through group discussion.
  d. Take a group vote.

_____ 3. A presentation given from brief notes is called
  a. extemporaneous.
  b. impromptu.
  c. manuscript.
  d. memorized.

_____ 4. What organizational plan would be best for an oral presentation in which a person is being introduced to an audience?
  a. Cause-Effect
  b. Direct or Indirect
  c. Problem-Solution
  d. Topics-Subtopics

_____ 5. Which of the following visual aids would best support an oral presentation in which a new product is being introduced?
  a. Audio tape describing the product
  b. Handouts explaining the product
  c. Model of the product
  d. Transparency picture of the product

_____ 6. Which of the following visual aids would best promote audience interaction in exploring alternatives?
  a. Movie
  b. Overhead transparency
  c. Poster
  d. Projection device visual

_____ 7. Which of the following is not an appropriate method for maintaining meeting records?
  a. Ask a group member to serve as recorder.
  b. Ask a support staff member to take notes.
  c. Elect someone to be a permanent recorder.
  d. Have the leader make notes after the meeting.

8. The purpose of a group will determine all but which of the following?

    a. How often the group meets

    b. How the group's work is accomplished

    c. Whether records are maintained

    d. Who should attend the meetings

9. Audio conferences use

    a. interactive cameras.

    b. microphones.

    c. pagers.

    d. telephone technology.

10. GDSS is an acronym for

    a. group decision support system.

    b. guided discussion software system.

    c. group development software solution.

    d. guided discussion speaker system.

Matching

In the blank to the left of the description, write the letter of the best answer. Answers may be used once, more than once, or not at all.

1. Can reduce cost, increase productivity

2. Problem solving; brainstorming

3. Natural; healthy

4. Inform, persuade, entertain

5. Foundation for a successful oral presentation

6. Read to an audience

7. No preparation time

8. Uses touch to reinforce

9. Given from notes

10. Platform or hand-held

    a. bullet

    b. conflict

    c. extemporaneous speech

    d. handouts

    e. impromptu speech

    f. manuscript speech

    g. microphones

    h. objects

    i. preparation

    j. presentation graphics software

    k. purposes

    l. research

    m. speaker

    n. video conference

Completion

Complete each item by writing the necessary word or words.

1. Knowing how to _____ and participate in meetings is essential to making them worthwhile, _____ experiences.

2. The _____ and _____ of a group must be well defined.

3. Meetings should be _____ or conducted in another format if no _____ need to be discussed or no _____ need to be made.

4. The _____ and related _____ should be distributed in advance of a meeting.

5. The leader should be sure that meetings _____ and _____ on time.

6. The first step in conflict resolution is to be sure the basic _____ is clear.

7. Lively debate is _____; arguments are _____.

8. When speaking to an established group within your organization, you should consider both _____ and _____.

9. When using transparencies, position the screen on a _____ and tilt it _____ the projector.

10. When using audio aids during a presentation, a speaker must be sure the _____ is high and the _____ is sufficient for all to hear clearly.

11. Presentation graphics software allows users to create _____, _____, _____, and _____.

12. Keep a presentation _____-centered by using the _____.

13. The four types of questions you might encounter during a question-and-answer session are _____, _____, _____, and _____.

14. Deflect hostile questions by _____ them before answering.

15. All presentations should end on a _____, _____ note.

Review Questions

1. What are the keys for successful meeting leadership?

2. What are your responsibilities as a participant in a meeting?

3. Explain why the extemporaneous style is best for business presentations.

4. What are the keys for effectively delivering an oral presentation?

5. List and briefly explain the alternatives to face-to-face business meetings.

6. What are the responsibilities of an event emcee?

7. What steps should you follow if asked to introduce a speaker?

8. In what ways should an emcee assist individuals who are to participate in a program?

9. What advice would you give to someone who planned to use handouts as a presentation aid?

10. What are multimedia aids? Give examples.

WORD PUZZLE

Across

1. another name for a small group
3. should permeate all meeting discussions
7. needed for a video conference
11. primarily responsible for success of a meeting
13. leader must keep group _____
15. insufficient reason for including someone at a meeting
16. number of ideas per visual aid
18. the purpose of a speaker introduction is to _____
20. status of meeting participants
22. presentation style rarely used in business
23. members should learn about the group's _____
24. permits anonymous comments during a meeting

Down

2. prepared by meeting leader
4. a spoken presentation is an _____ presentation
5. same as 1 Across
6. captures attention; introduces an item on a visual aid
8. _____ your audience
9. face-to-face is a type of meeting _____
10. most common presentation aids
12. good location for strategic planning meeting
14. use _____ carefully in a presentation
15. decide without voting; reach _____
17. not a substitute for content
19. you will do this during most of a meeting
21. ensures that an event begins, moves along, and ends on time